2/82

EVERGREEN PILOT BOOKS

Chief Editor
A. Norman Jeffares

Advisory Editors
David Daiches   C. P. Snow

ALBERT CAMUS

ALBERT CAMUS

Adele King

GROVE PRESS, INC.
NEW YORK

First published by Oliver & Boyd Ltd
Edinburgh, Scotland, 1964

Library of Congress Catalog Card Number: 64-1263

First Evergreen Edition 1964

Manufactured in Great Britain

CONTENTS

ACKNOWLEDGMENTS

For permission to quote from the copyrighted works of Albert Camus, acknowledgments are due to Librairie Gallimard, Hamish Hamilton Ltd., and Alfred A. Knopf Inc.

Acknowledgment is also due to *L'Express* (Paris) for permission to quote from Robert Kanters: "Camus: Prince des bien pensants ou de la révolte?"

The photograph on the front cover is reproduced by permission of Radio Times Hulton Picture Library.

A.K.

ABBREVIATED TITLES BY WHICH
CAMUS'S WORKS ARE CITED IN REFERENCES

All page-references not in brackets are to the original French text; all those in brackets are to the English translations listed here. For details of editions cited, see Bibliography.

C. = *La Chute* (*The Fall*, tr. J. O'Brien).

E. = *L'Etranger* (*The Outsider*, tr. S. Gilbert).

E.E. = *L'Envers et l'endroit*.

H.R. = *L'Homme révolté* (*The Rebel*, tr. A. Bower).

M.S. = *Le Mythe de Sisyphe* (*The Myth of Sisyphus*, tr. J. O'Brien).

N. = *Noces* (One essay "Summer in Algiers" is translated in *The Myth of Sisyphus*).

P. = *La Peste* (*The Plague*, tr. S. Gilbert).

CHAPTER I

BIOGRAPHICAL INTRODUCTION

Albert Camus was born in Algeria on 7 Nov. 1913. His father, a poor farm worker who had taught himself to read and write, was killed in the battle of the Marne in 1914. His mother, who had been left deaf and with a speech impediment by a childhood accident, was illiterate. After her husband's death she supported her family by long hours of work as a charwoman. Although there was little display of affection or communication between them, Camus's relationship with his mother was a deep and lasting influence on his life. His notebooks, which he began in 1935, open with a passage about his mother:

What I want to say: That one can have—without romanticism—the nostalgia for a lost poverty. A certain number of years lived in misery are sufficient to construct a sensibility. In this particular case, the bizarre feeling that the son has for his mother constitutes *all his sensibility*.[1]

The poverty and loneliness that Camus knew as a child did not leave any bitterness, and his memory of these early years helped to lay the foundation of his later thought. His childhood and youth were times in which the hardships of existence were amply balanced by a feeling of harmony with the natural world. Poverty was an aid towards focusing his view of existence; the misery and the happiness of human life stood out more clearly against a stark setting. Camus speaks of his youth in Algeria as the time when he found those "two or three great and simple images to which the heart first opened"[2] which form the underlying structure of all his work: the hot Algerian sun, the cool Mediterranean sea, and the silent, suffering mother.

In 1923 Camus won a scholarship to the *lycée* in Algiers, where he studied under the philosopher Jean Grenier. Grenier's humanism was influential for the development of Camus's thought. He taught Camus to be sceptical of abstract political ideologies, and Camus also attributed to him his awakening to a deeper sense of life:

> Personally, I had enough gods: the sun, the night, the sea. . . . Someone had to remind me of the mysterious and the sacred, of man's finitude and of his impossible love, so that I could one day return to my natural gods with less arrogance.[3]

Camus was also influenced by such pessimistic philosophers as Schopenhauer and Nietzsche. Articles that he wrote when he was still a *lycéen* show these influences. He had already decided that there was no rationalist explanation of the world; he sought some salvation in a world that seemed meaningless. Both in these early articles and later, Camus tends to use religious terminology, although he never accepted any religious system. ("I have," he was to say later, "a sense of the sacred, and I don't believe in a future life.")[4]

Later, intending to make a career of teaching, Camus studied philosophy at the University of Algiers. In the post-graduate thesis for which he was awarded a *diplôme d'études supérieures*, he describes how the early Christian church appropriated the philosophical forms and methods of the Neo-Platonists, particularly Plotinus. The thesis ends with a study of St Augustine, who successfully combined Neo-Platonic metaphysics and Christian doctrine.

Even in his thesis, there are hints of the problems with which Camus was trying to come to terms. In order to proselytise successfully among the Greeks, the early

Church had to reconcile its sense of the sin, terror, and irrationality of earthly existence with the Greek need to find coherence and order in the tangible world. Camus contrasts the two sensibilities: the Christian preoccupation with sin and with eternal salvation, and the Greek belief in innocence and in the importance of the natural world. These two outlooks parallel Camus's own sense of the dichotomy of existence as it is expressed in his first essay, *L'Envers et l'endroit*, published in 1937, the year after he presented his thesis. The world he describes is one in which death, strangeness, and loneliness often predominate, but in which man finds beauty and tries to give some meaning to his life. Camus would have agreed with the Greeks that "our kingdom is of this world" and with the Christians that this world is a place of tragedy, in which death is always imminent.

The preoccupation with death and salvation and the tenacious belief in the importance of the senses are undoubtedly reflexions of Camus's direct experience of the fragility of life, for at the age of seventeen he was attacked by tuberculosis; and the same disease recurred at several crucial moments in his life. A second attack, in 1937, prevented his passing the physical examination required of candidates for the *agrégation*.

Perhaps because of his early struggle against illness, Camus developed a strong sense of the necessity for self-domination and control:

It is a question of being quiet—of suppressing all that is public and of knowing how to judge oneself. Of balancing an attentive culture of the body with an attentive consciousness of living. Of abandoning all pretention and of applying oneself to a double task of liberation—with respect to money and with respect to one's own vanities and acts of cowardice.[5]

During the Second World War, when he was rejected for military service, he noted:

If they don't want me to fight, it's that I'm constantly being chosen to remain aside. And it is from this fight to stay a normal man in exceptional conditions that I have always drawn my greatest strength and my greatest usefulness.[6]

The years at the university and those immediately following until the outbreak of the War were, in spite of his illness, a period of considerable and varied activity for Camus. For several years he was a member of the Communist Party, and worked for it among the Moslems. He left the party in disgust over a shift in its policy towards the Arab population of Algeria. He wrote his first play, *Caligula*, and a novel, *La Mort heureuse*, which was never published, but which may be considered as a forerunner of *L'Etranger*. He read many of the authors who were major influences on his work:

Among the moderns: Grenier, Malraux, Montherlant. For the ancients: Pascal, Molière. Russian literature of the nineteenth century. The Spanish.[7]

Camus supported himself while at the university by various odd jobs, and was a member of a touring drama company sponsored by Radio-Algiers. The theatre and sports were continuing passions for him. Although he found groups of intellectuals unbearable, he could work happily with other people on the stage or in a stadium. These activities, within a closed world beyond normal moral concerns, became a means of recapturing the lost innocence of childhood. Camus helped to form a little theatre group in Algiers to bring drama to the working classes. He adapted several works for the stage, and contributed to a collectively-written play, *Révolte dans les Asturies*, based on the Spanish Civil War.

During his student years Camus made several trips to France, Italy, and Austria. The importance of travelling as a means of self-discovery is a theme of *L'Envers et l'endroit*, his first book of essays. In his notebooks of the period he speaks humorously of the difficulties of travelling when poor:

> It guards against dilettantism. I wouldn't say that what Gide and Montherlant lack is having reduced fares on the trains that force them to stay six days in the same city. But I know that I can't really see things as Montherlant or Gide did, because of reduced fares on the trains.[8]

The reflexions caused by his contact with another Mediterranean culture, that of Italy, are the basis for some of the lyric essays of *Noces*, Camus's second book. The ability of Mediterranean culture to counteract the excesses of northern pessimism remained a dominant theme in his work.

In 1937 Camus turned down a position at the college of Sidi-Bel-Abbès. This decision, as his notebooks show, was painfully difficult. He was torn between the need to earn a living and the more pressing need to avoid a situation in which his whole being might be numbed by monotonous routine. By 1938 Camus was able to earn a living as a journalist, another of the careers that he was to pursue intermittently throughout his life. He wrote literary and political articles as a reporter for the left-wing *Alger-Républicain*, and he became for a brief period editor of the evening edition of the paper.

Camus's most important work for the paper was a series of articles on the pitiable life of the Arabs in the Kabylia region. Although sometimes written in emotional language, these articles form a carefully-documented study of the injustice of the French administration towards the Arab population. They were written in 1939, but they are still useful for understanding the Algerian tragedy. Camus's basic position on the Algerian problem never changed. He felt that Algeria was a peculiarly mixed country, in which both French and Moslem populations needed full rights as citizens, and that a viable economy could only be achieved by continued association with France. Camus's insistence on preserving French ties was coupled with a demand for economic and social equality for the Moslem population.

The *Alger-Républicain* ceased publication after the outbreak of the War. Largely because of official hostility towards the left-wing and pro-Arab articles he had published, Camus could no longer find work as a journalist in Algeria, and Pascal Pia, the former editor of *Alger-Républicain*, helped him find newspaper work in Paris. After the German invasion Camus left for Lyons with the staff of *Paris-Soir*. In Lyons he married Francine Faure, and he returned with her to Oran. In 1942 he returned again to France, and as a result of the Allied landing in Algeria in November, he was separated from his wife for the remainder of the War. The separation of families and lovers became one of the dominant themes of *La Peste*, the novel which is partially an allegory of the German Occupation, and on which Camus was working from 1941 to 1947. *L'Etranger* and *Le Mythe de Sisyphe*, published in France in 1942, brought him sudden fame. They describe the "absurd" discrepancy between reality and man's desires.

In 1943, indignant because of the execution of a worker involved in a Communist uprising against the Nazis, Camus joined the Resistance movement "Combat." He became an editor of the movement's clandestine newspaper, again working with Pascal Pia. Camus contributed numerous unsigned articles to *Combat*, including two of his *Lettres à un ami allemand*, in which he stated the reasons for French resistance to the Occupation. These letters reject the nihilistic attitude that had tempted Camus since his early youth; they mark the point at which his work moves beyond the description of absurdity to the attempt to find a new basis for human values. The desire to go beyond nihilism is implicit in some of Camus's earlier work; in 1938 he had criticised Sartre's *Le Mur*, saying that a description of absurdity could only be a beginning, not an end. Nevertheless, the impact of the War years on Camus's thought, as on that of many philosophers who had accepted the relativity of all moral values, was to fortify the need to find a positive ethical basis for action.

Although its articles were mainly concerned with the fight against Vichy and the Nazis, in 1944 *Combat* began voicing its hope that some kind of socialism would be established after the War. What kind of socialism was not exactly defined, but important industries were to be nationalised and monopolies broken, while private business was to be allowed in less vital sections of the economy. The political parties of the old régime were scorned; *Combat* put its faith for the future in the "new men" revealed by the Resistance movement. The motto of the new *Combat*, which began open publication under Camus's editorship on 21 Aug. 1944, was "De la Résistance à la Révolution."

Camus was convinced that the half-truths of most newspapers contribute to social injustice. *Combat* was to be a major force in building a new France. Its first editorials reflect Camus's idealistic fervour and his hope that the experiences of the War had brought a new desire for liberty and justice to the French people. Camus became increasingly disillusioned as he found that the hoped-for revolution was thwarted by the return of the old politicians and of the old economic order. He was, as well, impatient of the normal workings of politics. Unwilling to devote his energies to a daily consideration of minor issues, he gradually withdrew from journalism. Although he continued to write occasional editorials, he gave up the editorship of *Combat* late in 1945. In after years he wrote only about a few clear-cut moral issues on which he placed great importance. He spoke out against aid to Franco, capital punishment, Russian suppression of the Hungarian revolt, and the terrorism and violence on both sides in the Algerian conflict.

The War years and those immediately following were Camus's most creative period. In 1943, in Lyons, he completed his second play, *Le Malentendu*, the bitterest and most nihilistic of his works. With the early play *Caligula*, *L'Etranger*, and *Le Mythe de Sisyphe*, it forms the "absurdist" phase of Camus's work, which was later balanced by the "rebel" phase of *Les Justes*, *L'Etat de siège*, *La Peste*, and *L'Homme révolté*, the books of the period after the War. Camus's notebooks show that, as early as 1940, he wrote with a conscious plan for a series of books that would reflect his view of life from varying angles. He began by describing "absurdity," a state of opposition between man and the universe that makes nonsense of normal moral values. Later he tried to formulate the moral rules that could be deduced from an awareness of "absurdity."

If *L'Etranger* expresses the moral *tabula rasa* of the War years, *La Peste* advocates revolt as a means towards creating a new moral consciousness. With the publication of *La Peste* in 1947, Camus was established as a major figure in post-war Paris. He became, to a degree that he found irritating, a moral mentor for the younger generation in France. His opinion was sought on many political issues, his name was wanted for various manifestoes. His books were greeted less as artistic works to be judged for themselves than as indications of the direction in which the author's thought was moving. The role into which he felt himself thrust was a constant source of uneasiness to Camus.

Although his plays are the least successful part of his creative work, Camus retained a passionate interest in the theatre. In the nineteen-fifties he made a number of highly skilful adaptations and translations for the theatre. Among these are Calderón's *Devotion to the Cross*, Lope de Vega's *The Knight from Olmedo*, Faulkner's *Requiem for a Nun*, and Dostoevsky's *The Possessed*. These perhaps show a greater talent for dramatic form and technique than Camus's own plays. At the Angers festivals in 1953 and 1957, Camus directed productions of his adaptations from Calderón and Lope de Vega and of his own *Caligula*. Late in 1959, shortly before Camus's death, André Malraux asked him to direct a new national theatre to produce classic and experimental plays. Camus seems to have turned increasingly to the theatre as a release from the tensions created by his position in the post-war literary world, especially after the publication of *L'Homme révolté*.

After a severe attack of tuberculosis in 1949, Camus withdrew from most public activity. During the next two years he completed *L'Homme révolté*, which produced a violent reaction in the literary and political press of Paris. The longest and most celebrated of the controversies was that between Camus and Sartre. Camus had earlier quarrelled with Sartre over the issue of slave labour in Russian camps; as the gap between their political views widened, an open break was perhaps inevitable.

The controversial articles appeared in Sartre's *Temps modernes* in April and August of 1952: a review of *L'Homme révolté* by Francis Jeanson, a reply by Camus, and rebuttals by both Sartre and Jeanson. The basis for the discussion was Jeanson's contention that *L'Homme révolté* was an idealistic work, which ignored the pressures of practical politics and the importance of the Communist movement as the only genuinely revolutionary force. Jeanson said that in seeking a pure rebellion not tainted by violence, Camus had removed himself from any effective action. Camus was neither on the right nor on the left, but "in the air." Camus replied that Jeanson ignored the major criticism of Marxism developed in *L'Homme révolté*: that the Communist revolution substitutes future goals for practical activity to alleviate present injustice and suffering. Neither Jeanson nor Sartre replied directly to this crucial thesis. The quarrel,

B

one of the major events of the French literary world since the War, is more important for the principles involved than for the quality of the arguments.

There were also controversies with André Breton and others on literary and political aspects of *L'Homme révolté*. In 1954 Simone de Beauvoir published a novel, *Les Mandarins*, based on the Sartre-Camus quarrel, and she presented Camus as an attractive but undisciplined figure who is willing to sacrifice principles for his personal pleasure. The bitterness of these quarrels weighed heavily on Camus's mind, and during the period 1952–56 he only published *L'Été*, a collection of lyrical essays most of which he had written earlier. When a new novel, *La Chute*, appeared in 1956, it reflected the break with Sartre. *La Chute* is written in an extremely brooding tone. It differs from Camus's other fiction in being set in the dark world of northern Europe. Although he lived in Paris for most of his adult life, Camus never resigned himself to the dreariness and darkness of the North. The hero of *La Chute* chooses to live in Amsterdam as a form of penance; he sees the city as a symbolic Hell.

Camus's withdrawal from political activity began with his disappointment in the post-war years. It was intensified after his disillusionment with the reception of *L'Homme révolté*. In the last years of his life Camus was often isolated because of his refusal to support either side in the Algerian rebellion. Unable to endorse the policies of the vast majority of European settlers in Algeria, Camus was equally unable to accept Algerian independence, which he felt would mean a sacrifice of the French population to the nationalists, whom he distrusted. He was appalled by the violence and terror in Algeria. In January 1956 he made a truce appeal in Algiers, demanding that both the French army and the F.L.N. should call a halt to acts of violence against the civilian population. Coming as it did when passions were aroused on both sides, Camus's plea for moderation had no effect. After the failure of this proposal, Camus said little about the Algerian problem. In 1958 he published a collection of his articles on Algeria, written between 1939 and 1958; he then refused to make additional public statements.

L'Exil et le royaume, a volume of short stories, was Camus's last creative work. These stories are less bitter, more objective renderings of Camus's mature reflexions on life. They perhaps indicate what was to have been a turning-point in his fiction: a movement away from political themes and towards greater realism and density of natural detail. The book on which he was working when he died, *Le Premier Homme*, was the first to which Camus referred as a "novel." Like Gide, Camus termed his earlier, more linear works "récits" or "chroniques." *Le Premier Homme* was to be part of Camus's third phase of work: a novel, a play (*Don Juan*), and an essay (*Le Mythe de Némésis*), all devoted to love.

In 1957 Camus was awarded the Nobel Prize for literature. With a part of his prize money, he bought a small house in Lourmarin in southern France, where he spent much of his time writing in an atmosphere more congenial and peaceful than that of Paris. On 4 Jan. 1960, while returning to Paris with a friend, Camus was killed in a car accident.

REFERENCES

1. *Carnets*, p. 15.
2. *E.E.*, p. 33.
3. Preface to Jean Grenier's *Les Iles*, p. 12.
4. Jean-Claude Brisville, *Camus* (1959), p. 260. See Carl Viggiani, "Albert Camus' First Publications" (1960).
5. *Carnets*, p. 107.
6. *Op. cit.*, p. 173.
7. Brisville, *Camus*, p. 259.
8. *Carnets*, p. 93.

CHAPTER II

FIRST ESSAYS

The short lyric essay was the first literary form adopted by Camus. It was in many ways his most natural means of expression. *L'Envers et l'endroit* (1937) and *Noces* (1938) are enthusiastic personal descriptions of the early experiences of people and of nature that formed the foundations of Camus's later work. Although his mature works have a classic discipline, they lack the open emotion of these early essays.

Camus was conscious of this discrepancy between emotion and order in his work. Although he later rejected the immaturity of expression in *L'Envers et l'endroit*, which he did not allow to be republished until 1958, he realised that it contained a passion sometimes missing in his work:

> To be built, a work of art must first use these obscure forces of the soul. But not without channelling them, surrounding them with dikes, so that their waves rise as well. My dikes, even today, are perhaps too high. Thus this stiffness, sometimes. . . . But the day when a balance is established between what I am and what I say, that day perhaps, and I hardly dare to write it, I will be able to build the work of which I dream . . . it will resemble *L'Envers et l'endroit* in one way or another and it will speak of a certain form of love.[1]

The "obscure forces of the soul" in *L'Envers et l'endroit* are those emotions that Camus felt as he came to grips with reality. The essays describe, haltingly sometimes, his first encounters with the tragedy of life, his first attempts to understand the duality of the world. The reflexions, although not as precise as in Camus's later essays, are intensely personal. As direct descriptions of a situation and of an emotion accompanying it, the essays of *L'Envers et l'endroit* occasionally attain a finely sensitive perceptivity.

The first essay, "L'Ironie," describes three encounters with age and loneliness. Camus takes an interest in an old woman about to die. Having become useless to her society, she has nothing upon which to rely but a vague hope in God, symbolised for her by a set of rosary beads and a cheap stucco statue. Camus understands the old woman's desperate need of his interest, but, at the same time, he feels a desire to slap her. Similarly, in a café he meets an old man trying to amuse a group of youths by his stories. Camus understands the loneliness of age. Unless the old man is recognised by others, he will feel dead. But Camus is too impatient to live his own life to give such sympathy to the old. The third encounter is between a child and his grandmother. The old woman dominates her family and frightens the child, who pretends to love her. She dramatises her illnesses to gain sympathy and to keep control of her family. When she dies the child feels as if her death were another comedy that she has arranged.

These short episodes are noteworthy for Camus's insight into the ambiguity of his reactions towards the old people. There is, especially in his description of his feelings towards his grandmother, a psychological penetration that he consciously banished from much of his later work. In "L'Ironie" he recognises his impatience with the demands of other people, but he also expresses clearly his natural sympathy and affection for the average man. This sympathy is based on a realisation that all life is tragic, and that even a coarse and ignorant person suffers. Sympathy for suffering is often so generalised or so controlled by irony in Camus's novels that it loses much of its force. "There is," he wrote in 1958 about *L'Envers et l'endroit*, "more real love in these awkward pages than in all those that have followed."[2]

Greater complexity of emotion and depth of love are expressed in the second essay, "Entre oui et non," a story of Camus's relationship with his mother. As a child, he finds his mother strange, silent and pitiful. Since he has been brought up by his domineering grandmother, there is no display of affection nor any communication between him and his mother. But in her complete silence and suffering, his mother embodies the immense indifference and solitude of the universe:

> He is sick to the point of crying in front of this animal silence. He pities his mother. Does that mean he loves her?[3]

When he is older, he is called to stay at her sick bed during the night. Lying beside her silent body, he feels that they are alone against everyone:

> He had never felt so lost. The world had dissolved and with it the illusion that life begins again every day. Nothing existed any longer, studies or ambitions, preferences at a restaurant or favourite colours. Nothing but the sickness and death into which he felt himself plunged.[4]

He is led, temporarily, to a resigned acceptance of this universe which is indifferent to suffering and to the fight for life:

> And tonight I understand how one can want to die, because, compared with a certain transparency of life, nothing has any importance.[5]

As a result of such encounters with human suffering and with the facts of aging and dying, Camus tries to find an attitude with which to confront the world. The elements of his experience appear to be irreconcilable. There is his own youthful desire for life and happiness, but there is also the certainty of death. He rejects religion; a belief in God is only a solace for those who have accepted death. "But let the hope of life be reborn and God will have no force against the interests of man."[6] His own plans for life suddenly seem meaningless. Of what use is it that he has grown up, since "accepting manhood leads only to being old?"[7] It is tempting to withdraw from the world of man; in nature there is the "indifference and the tranquillity of that which does not die."[8] As a child, in the cemetery, he responded more sincerely to the beautiful winter day and to the view of the sun over the bay of Algiers than to the death of his grandmother. And yet he cannot withdraw his pity. Indifference and stoicism cannot work in the face of the suffering he sees, or in the face of the certainty that he too will suffer and die. The world in itself seems simple: "It's men who complicate things."[9] Camus can find no answer to his puzzle except the resolve to look at life lucidly and to accept the whole of his destiny.

The next essays, "La Mort dans l'âme" and "Amour de vivre," approach this same puzzle about the duality of life through Camus's experience while travelling in Europe. Travelling to a strange country, where one is divorced from one's habits, one's friends, and even one's language, offers another vision of the incomprehensibility of life. The ordinary categories by which the mind understands are, temporarily at least, shattered.

The characters of Camus's fiction are usually self-confident; they revolt against the world because it does not satisfy their desires for happiness or clarity. If behind their revolt lies a period of anguish in which they questioned themselves as well as the world, this experience is not narrated. In the less guarded manner of such youthful essays as "La Mort dans l'âme" and "Amour de vivre," however, there is a description of the state that lies before revolt, even before lucidity, when a man's fear and inadequacy in the face of a strange situation tear down his defences, leaving him incapable of rebuilding on old ground. In Prague Camus writes:

> Man is face to face with himself; I defy him to be happy. . . . And yet this is how travelling enlightens him. A great discord occurs between him and external things. In this less solid heart, the music of the world enters more easily.

"But," he adds disarmingly, "do I need to confess that all this is only a story to put me to sleep?"[10]

Only later, in Italy, where he feels more at home in a Mediterranean landscape, can Camus attempt to rise above his despair by understanding it. In Italy the world is still indifferent to man; the sun shines on a landscape that offers nothing to man's aspirations. But the world is also beautiful:

> I needed some greatness. I found it in the confrontation of my profound despair with the secret indifference of one of the most beautiful landscapes in the world. Here I drew the force to be courageous and conscious at the same time.[11]

His response to beauty does not save man from the realisation of his mortality or his weaknesses, but it gives him courage to seek happiness and to accept his destiny without flinching.

A similar joy in the beauty of the external world occurs in Palma, at the cloister of San Francisco. Camus is afraid of being detached from his usual patterns of thought, of losing the routine that shields from him the strangeness of every moment. But, because his consciousness is suddenly drawn to immediate surface impressions, he sees a unique play of appearances. "We give to each being, each object, its value as a miracle."[12] The moment, the appearance, must be savoured, and is savoured more fully because one is conscious of impermanence:

There was all my love of life: a silent passion for what was, perhaps, going to escape me; a bitterness beneath a flame. . . . There is no love of living without despair about living.[13]

The emotion that inspires each of the essays is similar. An experience, such as pity for his illiterate, suffering mother, or despair at being unable to order a meal in Prague, cuts through Camus's normal acceptance of life. He questions the meaning of a world in which exist side by side death and beauty, suffering and joy, incomprehensibility and man's desire for clarity. Behind the uncertainty and despair described in *L'Envers et l'endroit* lies Camus's early, near fatal encounter with tuberculosis.

In a short concluding essay, "L'Envers et l'endroit," Camus attempts to draw a rule for living from his experiences. He formulates a view of life that is persistent throughout his work, and that causes him to oppose religion and, later, the major political and metaphysical ideologies of the contemporary world. "My kingdom," he realises, "is of this world."[14] It includes the play of the sun in a cloister in Palma, and the suffering of an old man trying to stay alive. It is a kingdom of the individual and the immediate, a kingdom of persons rather than of ideologies, a kingdom of sensations rather than of abstract knowledge. This kingdom is puzzling, it is a source of both joy and despair. We must live with the contradiction:

I hold to the world by all my gestures, to men by all my pity and my gratitude. Between these two sides of the world ("l'envers et l'endroit") I don't want to choose, I don't like anyone to choose. . . . Great courage consists in keeping your eyes open on the light as well as on death.[15]

In *Noces*, his second book of essays, Camus turns towards the light more than towards death. *Noces* has none of the embarrassingly personal tone that Camus felt

betrayed his experience in *L'Envers et l'endroit*. To avoid
sentimentality, Camus does not describe human weakness.
The man who opposes evil and suffering in the world is
never a pitiable protaganist; he is young and confident of
his power even when he is aware of his despair. *Noces*
celebrates the nuptials between man and the earth. It is a
hymn of praise to the beauty of the natural world and to
the courage of a man who finds happiness in a full,
sensual life and in a lucid appraisal of his destiny.

The strength of these essays lies both in the lyric
imagery and in a clear presentation of Camus's attitudes
towards life. The theme alternates between joy for the
harmony between the body and the earth, and scorn of
anything that detracts from a full enjoyment of the
present. Tipasa and Djémila, ruined Roman cities near
Algiers, are the settings for meditations in two moods.

"Noces à Tipasa" celebrates Camus's joyous discovery
of his gods: the sun, the sea, the flowers that have over-
run the ruins. Such gods are worshipped by the body. No
spiritual contemplation is needed: "In Tipasa, I see is
equivalent to I believe."[16] Camus feels an intense love
for the world, and is possessed by the desire to get as close
as possible to it, to feel the earth against his naked body,
to plunge into the sea.

In Djémila nature is not a warm sun and sea, but a
cutting wind that pierces Camus, polishing him as a
pebble, wearing him down to his soul. In "Le Vent à
Djémila" he describes the effect of this wind: "I have
never felt to such a degree at once my detachment from
myself and my presence in the world."[17] This detachment
from himself is similar to the experience that Camus
described as he lay through the night by his sick mother.
Then, however, he felt only despair at the power of
death. In Djémila he again feels the presence of death,
but he draws from this experience a new strength to live
in the present, to bear the weight of his own life. If death
can make nonsense of man's projects for the future, man

must refuse all ideas of "later" so as not to renounce the richness of the present. More especially, he must refuse any hope of an after-life; he must reject all illusions and all self-pity.

The external world at Djémila, where nature has re-conquered the monuments by which the Roman Empire hoped to endure, teaches Camus that there is no im-mortality. All that mankind can accomplish, the only progress that civilisation can make, is to "create men who die conscious."[18] Camus resolves to maintain this con-sciousness of death within himself. He will accept without joy the inevitable closed door of death, but he will desire to the end the "exalting images of a world for ever lost."[19] Camus finds in the wind and the barren stone a confirma-tion of the beauty and the despair that the world offers to man.

In "L'Eté à Alger" Camus describes Algerian life. Alger-ians unconsciously share Camus's rule of living in the present. Life for them is not something to construct but something to burn up while they are young. They know that life's happiness will be over by the time they are thirty: "They wagered on the flesh, but knowing they were to lose."[20] They live without myths and without consolations. Camus sees in the Algerians a creative, bar-barian people who may be able to erect a new culture capable of showing the greatness of man. This greatness lies in an ability to see that there is no meaning in the world and that happiness must be sought in temporary sensations:

Everything that exalts life at the same time increases its absurdity. In the Algerian summer I learn that one thing only is more tragic than suffering and that is the life of a happy man. But it may be also the way to a greater life because it leads to not cheating.[21]

Camus recognises that there is much suffering and little love in the lives of these poor people of Algiers whom he holds up as models. Yet in *Noces*, in contrast to *L'Envers et l'endroit*, he emphasises the dignity in their simple acceptance of life and in their instinctive horror of death. Camus's own approach is, of course, less instinctive. He has, however, found his truth through his emotions and only later defined it abstractly. He describes his reaction to death as "this physical fear of the animal that loves the sun."[22] His love of life is a series of immediate responses to the sun, the sea, and the bodies of Mediterranean women as they walk through the town.

Standing on a hill in Florence, looking at the Tuscan landscape, Camus can define his view of life. Because of his instinctive refusal to accept any truths but "those that the hand can touch,"[23] he rejects religion. He will let no "dead ideas" stand between him and his love of "that within us which will die forever."[24] He will find happiness in the beauty of the earth and in his "double consciousness of his desire to endure and his destiny in death."[25] His life will be built on revolt and consent: revolt against the tragic certainty of death, and consent to the earth— through which man finds the only purity he can attain.

Le Mythe de Sisyphe (1942), Camus's next essay, is another passionate plea for a life of physical fulfilment and for a constant awareness of death. Here Camus presents his ideas in a more philosophical manner. He sacrifices the direct descriptions of *L'Envers et l'endroit* and *Noces* in order to achieve a more universal formulation of the human dilemma. But *Le Mythe de Sisyphe* is not an essay in pure reason; if one can find flaws in the logical arguments it is because their foundations lie in the emotional discontent described in the earlier essays.

Le Mythe de Sisyphe begins with an assumption that life has no meaning. This assumption is based on such emotions as Camus felt when lying beside his sick mother or when standing in the wind at Djémila. None of the usual codes of behaviour, such as working to gain a good position in the world, has much sense in a universe that is indifferent to man and that promises only death. Given this feeling of ultimate despair, what course can man take? Perhaps suicide is the only reasonable answer. The old man in *L'Envers et l'endroit* to whom no one will listen, walks forlornly in the streets, hoping that tomorrow everything will change. Suddenly he realises that every tomorrow will be the same:

> And this irremediable discovery crushes him. Such ideas make you die. If you cannot endure them, you kill yourself.[26]

Camus enumerates a number of situations in which men are led to question the meaning of their existence. His examples parallel the experiences described in his earlier essays. He speaks of the moment when "the stage-sets collapse,"[27] when we suddenly question the routine of daily life that has carried us along. Why are we continuing? A man may also approach the absurd through a sudden rebellion of the flesh, when he realises that he is growing old, that all the tomorrows for which he hoped and planned are merely leading him towards death. Camus evokes the experience of external strangeness that he described in "Le Vent à Djémila":

> A step lower and strangeness creeps in: perceiving that the world is 'dense', sensing to what a degree a stone is foreign and irreducible to us, with what intensity nature or a landscape can negate us.[28]

Finally, the mere fact of death, its mathematical certainty, awakens a sense of life's futility.

The operations of the mind produce a similar feeling of absurdity. While Camus uses familiar logical paradoxes, his argument is again based on emotional discontent. Man wants to comprehend the world through a unifying principle; this desire for absolute knowledge can never be satisfied. We can know traits and appearances of ourselves and of other persons, but we can never seize an essence. Even our knowledge of objects is unsatisfactory. All we know of a thing is that it exists because we can touch it. We can, Camus says, know truths but never the truth. Camus's argument is not simply a restatement of usual epistemological problems. To questions of how we know and what facts we can establish, his answers would be similar to those of an empiricist. Within the realm where they are efficacious, he defends the use of reason, common sense, and scientific investigation. He never denies the reality of the external world as it is immediately apprehended by the senses. Such sensory experience is his basis for possible knowledge.

Camus's complaint that the world is ultimately unknowable is a more radical matter. It is, in fact, hard for us to imagine a world that could fulfil Camus's desire for clarity. Only in the "closed world" of art, where beings and objects are given a permanent and unchanging form, could such knowledge be possible. Later, in *L'Homme révolté*, Camus praises art because it gives some satisfaction to man's desire for absolutes. When Camus revolts against the approximate nature of all knowledge, his revolt is of the same order as his revolt against death. No human action could solve his dilemma; his revolt is bound to be ultimately sterile. It expresses, however, a romantic dissatisfaction with the order of the world.

This dissatisfaction is the basis of "absurdity" as Camus defines it. Camus's particular concept of "absurdity" is a key point in his philosophy; it is the foundation of his moral and artistic doctrine. It is not a characteristic of the external universe itself, but of the insoluble opposition between what is and what man desires:

This world in itself is not reasonable, that is all that can be said. But what is absurd is the confrontation of the irrational and the wild longing for clarity whose call echoes in the human heart. The absurd depends as much on man as on the world. For the moment it is all that links them together. . . . This is all I can discern clearly in this measureless universe where my adventure takes place.[29]

The truth upon which Camus builds is the experience of frustration that he first described in *L'Envers et l'endroit* at his meeting with the old woman:

He believed that truth existed and knew as well that this woman was going to die, without worrying about resolving this contradiction.[30]

All Camus's later thought is an effort to draw such meaning and value as can be drawn from this contradiction between desire and reality.

Camus is certain of the existence of three things: his own desire, a world that cannot satisfy it, and an absurdity arising from the confrontation of man and the world. These are the only certainties he has; the only way of life and of thought that does not cheat is one that maintains all three parts of this "odd trinity."[31] If we judge that the absurd is true, we must preserve it; it can only be preserved by a constant act of revolt. This revolt will be without hope (for the rebel is always aware of death), but without resignation (for he continues to rebel against death). Camus says that revolt follows logically from his description of the world. But it is not, of course, strictly logical to contend that: "If I judge that a thing is true, I must preserve it."[32] Rather the decision to revolt, to preserve the absurd confrontation of man and the world, is a moral decision. Camus makes this decision because he wants to move beyond nihilism. Revolt will provide a basis for making value judgments, even in a disordered world.

Camus criticises what several philosophers have deduced from the discrepancy between desire and reality. Often they suppress one of the terms of Camus's trinity.

Upon recognising the scandal and paradox of existence, Chestov and Kierkegaard decide to believe in a cruel and irrational God. They suppress man's desire for order. Their God demands the sacrifice of human intellect; desire for knowledge becomes a sin. On the other hand, such attempts as Husserl's phenomenology to explain the universe on rational terms suppress the incomprehensibility of reality. Reality, however, is not totally rational nor is it totally irrational. Any refusal to maintain the tension between man and the world, any denial of part of the paradox, results in what Camus terms "philosophical suicide."

There is perhaps a parallel between Camus's description of absurdity and Freud's insight into human neurosis. Absurdity results from an essential difference between the world and man's mind, which produces nostalgia for an unobtainable paradise. A cat, Camus says, cannot know absurdity because it is not conscious of any impossible desires. Similarly, for Freud, man is the only neurotic animal because he alone has repressed desires that are necessarily frustrated by the organisation of human life. The terms of the inquiry into the nature of man are, of course, radically different for Freud and Camus. Camus speaks only of the conscious frustrations caused by irrationality and death. His theory is, however, based upon his emotional discontent; his concept of absurdity is another formulation of the fundamental neurosis that is the human condition.

Suicide is a rejection of the game. Instead of finding life unacceptable because it has no ultimate sense, Camus insists that life can be better lived in an awareness of absurdity. He draws his description of this "absurd" life from the instinctive religion of revolt and consent of *Noces*. Lacking any transcendent values, the absurd man will realise that his kingdom is of this world, a kingdom of the present moment, the immediate sensation. Camus refers to this kingdom as the "hell of the present." His exuberant acceptance of the world of the senses is evident, however, in his description of this "hell":

> Abstract evidence retreats before the poetry of form and colours. Spiritual conflicts become embodied and return to the abject and magnificent shelter of man's heart. . . . The body, affection, creation, action, human nobility will then resume their places in this mad world.[33]

Camus draws three consequences from the decision to accept this earthly kingdom. Man must maintain a state of revolt by being conscious of the nature of the world while refusing to acquiesce in its tragedy. "Revolt" in *Le Mythe de Sisyphe* has a purely metaphysical meaning: "the certainty of a crushing fate, without the resignation that ought to accompany it."[34] Being conscious that death makes a mockery of all his plans, the rebel also finds a peculiar sort of liberty: the liberty of the condemned prisoner. Because there is no tomorrow, there is no point in setting goals, in choosing a role that in any way restricts one's freedom of action. Finally, because death is the most evident absurdity against which he revolts, man will realise his greatest victory by accumulating the greatest quantity of experiences. Quality of life is to be replaced by quantity of life. Even though it is a result of chance rather than will, sixty years of life is a greater accomplishment for the rebel than forty years. In his discussion, however, Camus effectively shifts his argument. All men, he says, have the same quantity of experiences in a given time. What matters is to be fully conscious of the experiences that life presents. Camus's argument for a quantitative life becomes a plea for a passionately conscious life.

Camus defines the "absurd" man as one who is always conscious of tragedy and death, free from any illusions either of eternal life or of the saving power of some goal within life, and passionately interested in accumulating

c

sensual experiences. He illustrates this life by various examples: Don Juan, the actor, the adventurer, the artist. Each of these absurd heroes has chosen to live in the present; each has no regrets for the past and no hope for the future. Don Juan sees love not as a long experience tending towards the eternal, but as an immediate sensation, which "recognizes itself to be both short-lived and exceptional."[35] The actor is also a ruler of a perishable kingdom of the present; like Don Juan he is constantly on the move, draining each experience, each role, fully.

Camus's adventurer is a vague figure; perhaps he can be understood as a forerunner of the rebel of *L'Homme révolté*. He is less a military leader than a revolutionary. But he is not bound by political doctrines; he is dedicated to securing immediate justice and happiness. The adventurer accepts the provisional nature of his conquests. He realises that all revolution is ultimately a metaphysical protest against the fate of man, and that against this fate no victory is final. Man is his own end, and man in his struggle has a greatness that makes him the equal of a god.

The artist creates for the adventure of creation. He exhausts his life in miming the diverse and marvellous experiences that the world of perception and emotion offers. If he is a painter or a musician, the artist recaptures the pure world of colour or sound. The novelist has a special problem. He is tempted to explain the world rather than simply to describe it. Camus maintains that such explanation should be renounced; the novelist should limit himself to illustrating the absurd confrontation between man and the universe. He should not raise hope in a rational explanation of the world or in an immortality that would justify man's suffering. If he is content to describe life, and if he remains aware that even art is gratuitous, that no fame can console him for his own death, the artist can be "the most absurd character."[36] Artistic creation allows him to clarify his revolt and to develop more fully those spiritual forces that give dignity to man.

The choice of any style of life is possible, as long as man is conscious of the gratuitousness of his action, of the "mad character"[37] of the role he is playing. If he were to take his role as meaningful, he would pretend that life was rational, and would elude part of the absurd dilemma. Camus praises the great nobility of those who maintain their rebellion: "Conquest or play-acting, multiple loves, absurd revolt are tributes that man pays to his dignity in a campaign in which he is defeated in advance."[38]

He ends the essay by presenting his version of the Sisyphus myth. Sisyphus is the absurd hero who despised the gods, hated death, and maintained a passion for life on the earth. For this he was sentenced by the gods to a meaningless and never-ending task. Yet, because he was conscious, he could retain his dignity and surmount his fate by scorn. He could respond with joy to sensual appearances. He could, as well, find happiness: "The struggle itself towards the heights is enough to fill a man's heart. One must imagine Sisyphus happy."[39]

Le Mythe de Sisyphe reaffirms the dignity and value of life. In spite of the atmosphere of nihilistic thought and despair that influenced his generation, Camus finds reasons to justify his instinctive desire for happiness and his love of life. More reasons for despair were developing, however, even while Camus was writing *Le Mythe de Sisyphe*. The powerful political ideologies of Fascism and Communism offered new threats to the quest for happiness. They posed questions of man's behaviour towards others that went beyond the personal perspective of *Le Mythe de Sisyphe*. After considering these problems for ten years, Camus published *L'Homme révolté*, his second major philosophical essay.

REFERENCES

1. *E.E.*, pp. 30–1.
2. *E.E.*, p. 13.
3. *E.E.*, p. 65.
4. *E.E.*, p. 69.
5. *E.E.*, pp. 70–1.
6. *E.E.*, p. 39.
7. *E.E.*, p. 67.
8. *E.E.*, p. 62.
9. *E.E.*, p. 76.
10. *E.E.*, pp. 88–9.
11. *E.E.*, p. 101.
12. *E.E.*, p. 109.
13. *E.E.*, pp. 112–13.
14. *E.E.*, p. 123.
15. *E.E.*, pp. 124–5.
16. *N.*, p. 22.
17. *N.*, p. 33.
18. *N.*, p. 36.
19. *N.*, p. 39.
20. *N.*, p. 45 (113).
21. *N.*, p. 62 (121).
22. *N.*, p. 35.
23. *N.*, p. 60.
24. *N.*, p. 79.
25. *N.*, p. 85.
26. *E.E.*, p. 48.
27. *M.S.*, p. 27 (18).
28. *M.S.*, p. 28 (19).
29. *M.S.*, p. 37 (24).
30. *E.E.*, pp. 37–8.
31. *M.S.*, p. 48 (31).
32. *M.S.*, p. 49 (31).
33. *M.S.*, pp. 74–5 (46).
34. *M.S.*, p. 77 (48).
35. *M.S.*, p. 102 (63).
36. *M.S.*, p. 125 (76).
37. *M.S.*, p. 140 (84).
38. *M.S.*, p. 129 (77).
39. *M.S.*, p. 168 (99).

CHAPTER III

THE REBEL AND THE ARTIST

If in *Le Mythe de Sisyphe* Camus examines the implications of "the absurd" for the individual, in *L'Homme révolté* (1951) he is concerned with the effects of rebellion against the absurd upon society. In both essays, Camus begins by assuming that there are no transcendental values, and then tries to establish, for an age without faith, a way to go beyond nihilism. Rebellion itself is the foundation of this search for values. In *Le Mythe de Sisyphe* Camus says that the hero of the absurd must preserve his individual consciousness in his rebellion against death. In *L'Homme révolté*, however, Camus claims that the political rebel prefers to die rather than to continue as a slave. Because he chooses to fight for justice rather than for his life, the rebel's action suggests that a man can value something beyond his own existence, something that he wants to share with other men. Revolt is based on a belief in a common human dignity. Unfortunately, in practice this belief is frequently destroyed.

According to Camus, the major political and intellectual problems of the modern world derive from this perversion of the spirit of revolt. To trace the history of revolt, Camus distinguishes between rebellion and revolution. Rebellion is an underdog's passionate uprising against his oppressor; it seeks an immediate goal and is best illustrated by the slave uprisings of antiquity. Revolution is a product of the modern mind. It is the rational use of terror to establish future justice. The revolutionary, in the name of some future goal, destroys the common bonds between men. According to Camus, the revolutionary mentality develops from attempts by artists, philosophers, and political thinkers to counter life's absurdity.

In *Noces* and *Le Mythe de Sisyphe* Camus says that in his personal opposition to the absurdity of the universe, revolt is balanced by consent. If he is dissatisfied, Camus also searches for happiness within the present; his revolt is limited by a realisation that the world is not entirely evil. In *L'Homme révolté* Camus compares this limit to the Greek sense of moderation, Greek rebellion was limited because the Greeks had no single, all-powerful God against whom to rebel.

Camus contrasts the Greek sense of moderation with modern metaphysical revolt as it appeared in Western culture in the eighteenth century. Modern revolt is not limited by any love of the world, rather it strives to transform the world and to oppose its cruel Creator. The first metaphysical rebels attack God, but they do not deny God's existence. Camus interprets this cruel God as the Judaic God of the Old Testament. He sees Christ as a great mediator, who was to reconcile God and man, and to solve the problems of death and evil by His suffering. Christ would thus remove the causes of rebellion. But the Church refused to recognise Christ's full role. By condemning those Gnostic heresies that stressed Christ's function as a mediator, Christianity became closely allied with a God of vengeance; grace became arbitrary, and God was again the inexplicable enemy of man. The beauty of nature was denied, and nature became the theatre in which to stage the history of divine punishment and salvation.

Modern metaphysical rebellion is inseparable from this Christian tradition. Camus's critique of metaphysical revolt in modern times begins with a study of the Marquis de Sade. Sade was in the tradition of libertine thought that destroyed the last remnants of Christ's role as redeemer. The libertines denied the divinity of Christ, who seemed to them only another human being suffering at the hand of a cruel and incomprehensible God. Sade sees innocence and virtue punished, crime rewarded, and in this proof of God's cruelty he finds a justification for the cruelty of man. Sade's cruelty is expressed in an unbridled sexual licence and in a will to power; other persons are reduced to the role of objects, to be enjoyed and to be destroyed. But the will for destruction can never be satisfied. Sade wants the annihilation of the world, even if he too must die. Sade's work illustrates, according to Camus, that an unlimited revolt, which begins by proclaiming absolute liberty, ends in the "desire for the apocalypse" and in the destruction of man.

Camus traces a similar tendency to move from a desire for unlimited freedom to a desire for total destruction in some of the most influential nineteenth-century philosophers and poets. According to him, metaphysical revolt fails when the rebel forgets the tension which arises because his desire to remake the world is subject to the narrow limits imposed by his love of concrete individual things and by his inability to change the nature of reality. The rebel demands recognition of his rights against God, but he realises that he cannot become God. At the same time, the rebel's acceptance of the world is limited by a consciousness of his dissatisfaction; he never lets consent to the world degenerate into a banal conformity.

The Romantic poets are an early example of revolt against evil and injustice being turned into a desire to do evil. To the Romantics, good appears as a weapon in God's hands, which He uses for His unjust designs. To rebel against God's injustice, they must defy His law. They realise, however, that they are not powerful enough to defeat God. The Romantic poet, unable to "do," turns all his attention to "appearing." He becomes a dandy, and acts out his life in front of the mirror of public opinion. "He plays at life because he is unable to live it."[1] Dandyism is a reply to God; it is an attempt to talk to Him as an equal, an equally evil, creature. Another stage in the development of modern revolt is reached with Dostoevsky. If the dandy defies moral law, Ivan Karamazov denies that moral law exists in a world based on injustice and arbitrary grace. From his revolt against injustice, Ivan draws the principle that "Everything is permitted." To be consistent, Ivan must force himself to do evil. Camus sees in this attitude the beginning of the attempt by later revolutions to kill God and remake the world.

In Lautréamont's litany of evil, *Les Chants de Maldoror*, Camus sees a revolt similar to that which animated the Romantics:

> He rebels against the injustice done to himself and to man. But in the moment of lucidity when he perceives at the same time the legitimacy of this revolt and its impotence, the fury of negation spreads even to that which he wants to defend.[2]

Lautréamont wishes to annihilate the world and his own consciousness. His revolt becomes an absolute "no." Camus reads Lautréamont's later work, *Les Poésies*, as an absolute "yes," an acceptance of the world as it is, and a return to the most banal kind of conformity after the failure of revolt. This, too, is a betrayal of the tension of the true rebel.

Camus's discussion of Nietzsche shows the extent of his debt to Nietzscheian thought. Nietzsche, as Camus interprets him, is less a prophet of nihilism than a clinical analyst of his time. Nietzsche accepts the death of God as a fact of his world, and tries to find a way for man to live in a world without belief. In Camus's description of Nietzsche's method, we can see what Camus himself attempts to do in *Le Mythe de Sisyphe* and in *L'Homme révolté*:

> The 'Can one live as a rebel?' became with him 'Can one live, believing in nothing?' His reply is in

the affirmative. Yes, if one creates a system out of absence of faith, if one accepts the final consequences of nihilism, and if, on emerging into the desert and putting one's confidence in what is going to come, one feels, with the same primitive instinct, both pain and joy.[3]

This primitive instinct of pain and joy is the dual attitude of Camus's rebel. In the desert of nihilism, Nietzsche, like Camus, rejects all transcendent values, which are only ways of hiding the real world from man. The absence of *a priori* values does not mean unbridled liberty, since with no laws, man must make his own order, must create his own greatness. Nietzsche finds this greatness in an "absolute assent, a complete and exalted allegiance to this world."[4] The only divinity is the Earth.

The young Camus of *Noces* was greatly influenced by Nietzsche's thought. But having seen in what ways Nietzsche could be used by the Nazis as an apologist for racist theories and for unlimited violence, Camus is forced to look again at Nietzsche to see if he betrays the concept of revolt that Camus hopes to use as his own method of going beyond nihilism. He finds that Nietzsche, in his absolute assent to what is, neglects the negative pole of revolt, the moment of pain. He accepts everything, even suffering, in a noble attempt to reach an inner blessedness. This acceptance, when divorced from Nietzsche's force of character, lends itself readily to a justification of making others suffer. Nietzsche's concept of an historical evolution towards some future superman also justifies sacrificing the present to the future; like Marx's theory of the classless society, it can be used to replace the value of "what is" by "what is to come." Both theories help to usher in the deification of history.

Camus's analysis of political rebellion in the modern world is based on movements of thought rather than on material causes. His neglect of economic and social factors in *L'Homme révolté* has often been criticised. Camus, however, is not writing a comprehensive political history. He wants to show the importance of ideology in shaping the course of history. If we accept that Fascism and Communism developed as they did because of the thought underlying them, we will find in *L'Homme révolté* a stimulating interpretation of the dangers inherent in philosophical attempts to remake the world.

According to Camus, the leaders of modern revolutions of principle, instead of demanding equal rights, try to inject a new idea into the course of history. The first modern revolution was the French Revolution, whose leaders believed in the substitution of the sovereignty of the People for the divine sovereignty of the King. Drawing upon Rousseau's *Social Contract*, the French revolutionaries affirmed the sacred sovereignty of the General Will, which was infallible and indivisible. They inaugurated a reign of formal, abstract law. Saint-Just, whom Camus sees as the most heroic exponent of this new ethic, dreamed of an ideal country, unified in its pursuit of virtue. But men are not naturally virtuous, and factions arose. "A day comes when ideology conflicts with psychology."[5] The rule of law was shaken; Saint-Just, with continued faith in his principles, drew the logical conclusion that all who criticise the state are traitors. Thus the Terror was established. With it began the modern era when the State, as the supposed repository of justice, claims the right to suppress its critics by any available means.

The principles of justice and liberty proclaimed by the French Revolution were not a concrete morality, but a set of vague, transcendental values. These could easily be perverted or used hypocritically to provide an alibi for the *bourgeoisie* of the nineteenth century. Freedom was

the freedom of privilege consolidated by the police; the family, extolled by the conservative newspapers,

was supported by social conditions in which men and
women were sent down the mines, attached to a com-
munal rope; morality prospered on the prostitution of
the working classes.[6]

On what values could man rely if formal morality was
seen to be hypocritical? The major answer of the twentieth century, according to Camus, is the incorporation
of value into the flux of history. Values are no longer
pre-existing means of judging actions and making
choices, but goals to be realised in the future. As existing
values lose their status, human nature is denied. Man
becomes only an adventure, creating himself for some
future perfection.

The Hegelian dialectic is the major source of the
tendency to place all value in a state of "becoming."
Such a dialectic, Camus claims, leads to a reign of terror,
as did the moralistic attitude of Saint-Just:

At the beginning, everything, according to Saint-Just,
is an idyll, while, according to Hegel, it is a tragedy.
But in the end that amounts to the same thing. Those
who destroy the idyll must be destroyed or destruction
must be embarked on in order to create the idyll.
Violence, in both cases, is the victor.[7]

Since 1789 revolutionaries, like the metaphysical
rebels, want to equal God. The great difficulty, and
Camus returns to this point frequently in his discussion
of the major political movements of our time, is that man
is not capable of being God. Revolutions begin by deny-
ing the fundamental weaknesses of human nature, by
expecting too much of man. But men, in the diversity of
their needs and passions, are certain to oppose to some
extent the march of history as it is interpreted by those in
power. Revolutions become puritanical and seek to suppress what is best as well as what is weakest in men. All
revolutions lead to some form of slavery, in which men are
made to feel guilty, rather than divine.

Camus devotes only a few pages of *L'Homme révolté* to
Fascism, "the irrational terror." He sees the Fascist movement as purely irrational and nihilistic, glorifying nothing
but efficiency for its own sake. Because Camus does not
discuss the philosophy underlying the German identification of the self and the state, his analysis of Fascism as an
ideological threat to Western civilisation is one of the
weaker sections of his study. Camus is primarily interested
in what he considers a more serious menace, the "rational
terror" of the followers of Marx.

Camus sees Marx as an admirable figure, especially in
his moral denunciations of *bourgeois* hypocrisy. Marx,
however, combined a valuable critical method with a
Utopian messianism, which was the product of the very
Christian and *bourgeois* mentality that he sought to combat. Camus terms this mentality "Nordic"; he contrasts
it with the "Mediterranean" world view of the ancient
Greeks. In the Nordic outlook, based ultimately on the
Judaic view of history, the world evolves according to a
unique historical pattern; man must work out his salvation or his damnation during the course of history. The
natural world is only a stage for this drama. The Greeks
had a cyclical view of history, and they saw external
nature as an object of beauty with which man must feel
in harmony. (This distinction between "Nordic" and
"Mediterranean" world views helps Camus to define his
own position at the end of *L'Homme révolté*. While Camus
shares Christian preoccupations with death and suffering, he does not accept an eschatological view of history.)

Because of this Nordic-Judaic outlook, Marx is led to
find a sacrificial suffering figure who can save the world.
The proletariat serves to fill this role; it becomes more
and more humiliated and disgraced until in the revolution it redeems society's guilt. Those who hold to this
theory must logically approve of social measures that
increase the misery of the working classes and bring them
nearer their moment of suffering and triumph. Marx's

willingness to sacrifice the present for some golden age in the future is, for Camus, the most dangerous aspect of his doctrine.

Camus says that Marx's predictions about the course of economic history have been proved false by twentieth-century technology. If Marx as an economic prophet has already been superseded, what faith, Camus asks, can we have in his future classless society? What evidence is there that Russia is moving towards perfection? The concept of such perfection only has meaning within a religious universe. In a secular world, the attempt to usher in a new Eden results in the degradation of man. In some very moving pages of *L'Homme révolté* Camus describes the negation of human nature in a totalitarian society. Any artistic or scientific genius that does not fit into the pre-conceived movement of history is denied. History itself must be rewritten if it contradicts the present pattern of power. The revolution becomes, by a perversion that betrays Marx's own moral insight, an instrument of mystification; the working classes are as badly oppressed as they were by the nineteenth-century alliance of *bourgeoisie* and Church. The finest passions of man—love, friendship, his response to the beauty of nature, his respect for truth—are denied. Because of an essential flaw in their logic, modern revolutionaries, in attempting to create a future perfection, have created a present Hell.

Camus's criticism of Russian society is partially balanced by a denunciation of the West, which pursues a policy of production for its own sake. With such a dynamic, justice is postponed, and man is oppressed in favour of the machine. Work loses more and more of its creativity and dignity. In spite of greater personal freedom in the West, Western economic evolution leads to a denial of the full grandeur of man.

Although he criticises most revolutionary movements, Camus mentions one group, "the fastidious assassins,"

who embodied the true spirit of revolt. This small band
of Russian terrorists, in 1905, murdered to advance the
cause of justice for men, but they recognised the paradox
of their position. They exercised great respect for the
lives of others, refusing to kill unnecessarily; they also
believed that they could only redeem their action by
being willing to pay with their lives for those whom they
killed. They held that political violence was both necessary and unjustifiable. Their attitude contrasts with the
revolutionary's justification of violence and with the
bourgeois denial of its necessity. This paradoxical attitude
towards violence shows the tension of true rebellion; the
"fastidious assassins" rebelled against injustice in the
world, and yet they consented to the value of human life.
Their willingness to die signified their refusal to place
their revolution above the dignity of man.

Camus's admiration for these "fastidious assassins"
has often been ridiculed as an ineffectual romantic
attitude. No revolution would be possible, it is argued, if
every revolutionary who took a life had to pay with his
own. Perhaps, and yet the example of these fastidious
terrorists has an obvious appeal in an age that has begun
to grow accustomed to mass murders and political crimes.
They refused to see political revolution as an adequate
principle for the whole of a man's life. Camus dramatises
their story in *Les Justes*, and their example helps him to
formulate his own moral position.

In the concluding pages of *L'Homme révolté* Camus
attempts to find a valid basis for moral choices in a world
of the absurd. This basis cannot be abstract ethics, nor
can it be a worship of history; it is found in revolt itself.
The initial movement of revolt creates a sense of community among men—"I revolt, therefore we are"—
based on the realisation that one rebels in the name of
some dignity common to all men. The solidarity established by rebellion has, Camus claims, an ontological
status midway between an historical principle and an

abstract ethic. Solidarity is not an abstract virtue, because it is discovered in the midst of reacting to an unjust historical situation, but solidarity implies a human nature that transcends particular historical circumstances. From solidarity, Camus deduces other fundamental moral rules. Solidarity implies a communication among men; dialogues are not possible between masters and slaves; therefore slavery, or any injustice that enslaves some men, kills the dialogue, and must be rejected. Murder and violence also kill the dialogue; therefore murder must be avoided. However, since the refusal to use violence means consent to the world's imperfection, murder is sometimes necessary. Murder must be an exceptional act, the limit to which a man can go only once; to show his recognition of the dignity of life, the assassin must be willing to die.

Rebellion, Camus claims, should be based on the acceptance of limitations. Violence should be limited by an awareness of the value of human life; consent to the existing world should be limited by a refusal to accept injustice. The rebel guards a measure between saying "yes" and "no" to the world.

Camus's idea of measure is drawn primarily from two sources. The first source is a recognition of the imperfectibility of man. By contrast, all political ideologies neglect human psychology. Starting with a principle of absolute human innocence, ideologies end by supporting systems based on absolute guilt. Only by recognising that men cannot be made into gods, Camus says, can we create conditions in which men will be fully human. If, for example, we realise that our knowledge is always relative and limited, we shall reject aspirations to chart the course of history. Similarly, a recognition of man's irrationality, of the unjust passions of the human heart, will make us understand the necessary limits to a rational ordering of society.

The second source of Camus's concept of measure is

the dual attitude towards the world which is persistent throughout his work. In *Noces* it is described as a revolt against death and a consent to the earth. In *Le Mythe de Sisyphe* the absurd hero is constantly aware of his dissatisfaction, but he is also aware of pleasure. The world always offers man two faces; it is a place of exile in which he is an outsider, and it is a kingdom in which he seeks happiness. In *L'Homme révolté* the response to this world is defined as "Mediterranean thought." It is a balance between nature and history, between the world to which man consents and his attempts to change that world.

In all his work Camus attempts to combine a Greek acceptance of nature and a Christian dissatisfaction with man's condition. His attitude can be foreseen in his university thesis, where his sympathy lies with the Greek desire to find measure and order in the world, but his sensibility is often attuned to the early Christian concern with death and suffering. This ambiguous attitude is at the root of his philosophy. In *Le Mythe de Sisyphe* Camus expresses a romantic dissatisfaction with the world quite alien to Greek thought. But he defines absurdity as a magnificent struggle between man and the world, a struggle that he wants to preserve. This acceptance of the conditions of man's life is close to a Greek outlook, and it contrasts with the discontent with which Camus begins. Similarly, although Camus calls the limited revolt of *L'Homme révolté* a Mediterranean attitude, it is in reality a rather uneasy synthesis between a Greek ideal and a Nordic discontent. Camus's rebellion begins as a challenge to the hostile universe; it becomes an attempt to find an harmonious relationship with the existing world. The seeming inconsistencies in Camus's logic are often a result of this attempt to balance two outlooks. Much of his emotional power, in the essays as well as in his fiction, derives from this dual attitude towards life, which embodies a persistent duality in Western civilisation.

Camus says that efficacious political action will begin

with reality rather than with ideology. True revolt will not seek absolute justice or impossible liberty. It will seek approximations of its goals, and will make certain that the means towards these goals do not conflict with human solidarity. The rebel, recognising the relativity of his knowledge, will not sacrifice living men to some ideal future. The only example of such revolt that Camus mentions is militant trade unionism. The only political objectives of which he speaks are the abolition of capital punishment and the reorganisation of manual labour so that it again becomes creative.

The reader of *L'Homme révolté* may feel that the long analyses of revolutionary thought and action have only led to a reaffirmation of moderate, humanitarian liberalism, for which few immediate projects are specified. The essay was a profound disappointment to many of Camus's left-wing readers; his idea of rebellion was considered too tame and uninspiring. In *L'Homme révolté*, however, as in *Le Mythe de Sisyphe*, Camus wants to clear the ground for making reasonable moral choices; he refuses to construct an elaborate philosophical system of his own. If Camus can do little more than give examples of personal styles of living or suggest limited goals for which men in society can strive, these attempts in themselves might be considered useful correctives to the despair and cynicism of the present. Both books show that other moral systems, besides an Existentialist Christianity or a worship of power politics, can be developed from a sense of life's absurdity. In *L'Homme révolté*, as in *Le Mythe de Sisyphe*, however, Camus attempts to prove by logic what is basically an emotional conviction. His vision of life is useful for criticising other metaphysical and moral views, but it is ultimately a moral choice rather than a logical deduction.

Since he is primarily an artist, Camus places great importance on the relationship of art to rebellion. Revolt, as Camus defines it in *L'Homme révolté*, is a process of

D

creation rather than destruction, and art, as a creative force, is a part of true revolt. The artist, like the rebel, lives between consent and despair. He accepts and describes external reality. But he reshapes the world in his work, to give it the coherence and perfection that it lacks.

Camus says that the novel is historically linked to rebellion; it came to prominence in the eighteenth and nineteenth centuries, during a time of political upheavals. The novel translates to an aesthetic plane the same desire to remake the world that motivates revolutions. The novelist takes the flux of daily life as his subject-matter, but through his art he transforms the real world into a better world. Better, however, means not different, but more unified. Men suffer, in life, because they cannot perfectly know themselves or others; a life only takes a completed shape after death. Even our strongest passions do not have the permanence that we desire. Man's nostalgia for absolute knowledge or enduring love is always confronted by the changeable, incoherent nature of reality. In the novel this nostalgia can be realised:

> What, in fact, is a novel but a universe in which action is endowed with form, where final words are pronounced, where people possess one another completely and where life assumes the aspect of destiny? The world of the novel is only a rectification of the world we live in, in pursuance of man's deepest wishes. For the world is undoubtedly the same one we know. The suffering, the illusion, the love are the same. The heroes speak our language, have our weaknesses and our strength. . . . But they, at least, pursue their destinies to the bitter end.[8]

Camus says that the novel should be midway between formalism and realism. By this he means that the novelist should strive for a rigorously controlled form and that he should consider the whole realm of human experience as his subject-matter. He should not reduce man to his outward gestures, or deny the importance of the body. He should not neglect the beauty of nature or the tragedy of human history. The contemporary novelist, in order to give artistic expression to the vital forces of his era, should move beyond individual passions to the problems raised by the metaphysical and political revolutions of the twentieth century. Here Camus follows in the tradition of Dostoevsky and Malraux; he is concerned, not with individuals in relation to normal society, but with those extreme situations in which man is confronted with metaphysical anguish or with the terrors of violent political action.

The form and style of the novel, Camus believes, show the artist's protest against the existing world. The greater the classicism and control, the more effective this protest will be. Camus praises the French classical novelists for their effort "to give to the cries of passion the order of a pure language."[9] A classical restraint of language and of theme is a way for the artist to dominate his own emotion and the confusion of the external world. The classical artist has one basic experience to communicate and he limits himself to variations on this theme. "To be classical is to repeat oneself." Of Mme de La Fayette, Camus comments: "The plot and characters are limited in general to this idea and . . . everything is arranged to make it re-echo indefinitely."[10]

In *L'Homme révolté* Camus approaches the subject of artistic form through a discussion of sculpture. The sculptor generalises from the particular, idealises the imperfect, and gives stability to the flux of life. Similarly the novelist creates characters who rise beyond their individuality to become universal types. These characters are

similar enough to us that we can recognise them, but carried above us, enlarged by suffering which fixes their attitudes in our memory and makes them finally exemplary.[11]

The novelist creates characters who are capable of experiencing their passion with a consistency impossible in real life; they can live through a metaphysical idea to its logical conclusion.

According to Camus's theory, the novelist seeks a particular situation that can symbolise the universal human condition. His symbols should be rooted in an observation of concrete reality; they must not lend themselves to simplified allegorical schemes. But the symbolic representation of life can be stylised and exaggerated. This stylisation is a sign of revolt against the world. Such a conception of plot and character as limited, repetitive, stylised, having a consistency that contradicts the incoherent nature of reality, is opposed to the traditional view of the novel as a portrait in depth of individuals in society. It is this lack of complexity and individuality that is frequently criticised in Camus's work. To some extent, such criticisms result from a confusion between allegory and stylisation.

The novel, for Camus, is symbolic and concerned with a philosophical outlook on life. The novelist should not, however, try to preach. In *Le Mythe de Sisyphe* Camus makes a distinction between the thesis novel, which seeks to prove a set of ideas, and the philosophical novel. The philosophical novel is based on pragmatic knowledge of the world and on a metaphysical view that is never fully expressed. It contains "a whole implied existence, the wealth of which is suspected."[12] Camus insists, as well, that since all thought is provisional, an artist's views will evolve. Each work will reflect his thought at a certain point in his experience. A later work will show the limitations of his earlier philosophy, or it will perhaps suggest a different way of looking at reality. By understating his themes, and by expressing in his works the changes in his outlook, the novelist can avoid being didactic.

Irony is another weapon with which the artist combats didacticism. Irony enables him to avoid the danger of moving from a moral concern to a moralising attitude. By means of irony he can create characters with whom he feels in sympathy and yet not make them exemplars. The novelist forces himself to speak of his most passionate concerns and experiences in a controlled and humorous manner. "The best way to speak of what we love is to speak of it lightly."[13]

On a more philosophical level, artistic form, as Camus conceives it, is ironic. The unified form by which the artist expresses his rebellion against the world is a mocking gesture of protest. The novelist knows that the shape he gives to his private universe will not change the formlessness of the real world. Artistic creation is the endless task of a Sisyphus aware that his work is gratuitous. Like the measured rebellion advocated in *L'Homme révolté*, art teaches man that he is human and not divine.

REFERENCES

1. *H.R.*, p. 73 (48).
2. *H.R.*, p. 108 (section omitted in English edition).
3. *H.R.*, pp. 88–9 (58).
4. *H.R.*, p. 96 (64).
5. *H.R.*, p. 166 (103).
6. *H.R.*, p. 248 (171).
7. *H.R.*, pp. 171–2 (108).
8. *H.R.*, pp. 324–5 (231–2).
9. "L'Intelligence et l'échafaud," p. 219.
10. *Op. cit.*, p. 220.
11. Foreword to Louis Guilloux's *La Maison du peuple*, p. 15.
12. *M.S.*, p. 135 (80–1).
13. *L'Eté*, pp. 101–2.

CHAPTER IV

L'ETRANGER

L'Etranger (1942), Camus's first novel, is a narrative told by Meursault, a young French Algerian. The novel begins with the death of his mother, which he announces in a strikingly laconic manner: "Aujourd'hui maman est morte." This discrepancy between tone and subject-matter foreshadows Meursault's lack of conventionality. On his return from the funeral, he goes swimming and to the cinema with Marie, a young woman whom he knows casually, and that night he begins a love affair with her. During the next few weeks Meursault works as usual and sees Marie on Saturdays. He turns down his employer's offer of a position in Paris. Although he doesn't love Marie, he agrees to marry her.

Meursault's calm routine is disturbed by his friendship with Raymond, a young man thought in the neighbourhood to be a procurer. Raymond suspects his Arab mistress of infidelity and wants to punish her. Quite casually, Meursault is brought into the affair; he agrees to arrange a meeting between Raymond and his mistress. After Raymond beats her, her screams summon the police; Meursault makes a false deposition for Raymond. Without any personal motive he becomes enmeshed in the ensuing struggle between Raymond and his mistress's brother and friends. At a Sunday outing on the beach a fight breaks out and Raymond is wounded. Later Meursault walks alone on the hot beach, seeking shade from the sun, and he encounters one of the Arabs armed with a knife. Meursault, who has been entrusted with Raymond's revolver, is confused by the blinding light. He mistakes the reflexion of the sun for a flash of the knife blade, and he fires, killing the Arab. He then fires four shots into the dead body.

Meursault is imprisoned, tried, and sentenced to be hanged for murder. The jury's decision is based not on the nature of the crime itself (the murder of an Arab by a Frenchman would not normally have been a capital offence in Algeria), but on its appraisal of Meursault's character. Before the trial, Meursault refuses to give the examining magistrate any motive for the crime, except that he shot "because of the sun." He refuses to repent, admits that he has no belief in God, and gives an honest account of his activities during and after his mother's funeral: activities that, in the eyes of the *bourgeois* society judging him, do not show appropriate filial grief. The prosecuting attorney convinces the jury that Meursault is a "moral monster" who has neither normal emotions, nor any sense of guilt or sin. Imprisoned and awaiting execution, Meursault accepts his role as a social monster. When the prison chaplain tells him to repent and to prepare his soul for immortality, Meursault becomes angry; he defends the life that he has led, a life with no transcendent value, absurd in itself, but which is the only value to which he can cling. In accepting his life and his death, Meursault finds a strange peace and a sense of harmony with the external world.

A reading of *L'Etranger* becomes largely an interpretation of Meursault's character as it is shown in the form and style of his narrative. On this basis, one's initial reaction is that, according to the normal conventions of autobiography, Meursault is indeed an "outsider." He presents events and his reactions to them without analysis; he spends more time on trifling details and on sensory impressions of seemingly little value than he does on examining his own emotions. In telling how he wrote the letter that precipitated the chain of events leading to the murder, Meursault says nothing of his feelings about

Raymond's plan, but he describes in detail the objects in the room. In prison, Meursault's pastime is to remember his previous life; he thinks back, not on important events or emotions, but on each object and its position in his flat.

Meursault appears on the surface to be strangely indifferent to all normal motivations. Although he wishes his mother had not died, he feels no strong sense of grief. He is fond of Marie's laughter and he desires her, but he does not love her. Because he has no ambitions to better himself, he refuses a promotion: "anyhow, one life was as good as another and my present one suited me quite well."[1] He even maintains a certain distance from his trial; occasionally it interests him as a stage production; at other times he is completely indifferent and bored, wishing only to return to his cell to sleep. His only articulate expression of deeper feelings comes just before his death, when he expresses his love of life and his rejection of transcendent values.

At first glance, Meursault seems the opposite of the absurd hero. He does not appear to confront the absurd with lucidity. Rather, he appears indifferent to problems of importance, and contented with a banal daily routine. In *L'Envers et l'endroit* Camus projects a novel in which his heroes seem to be unconscious creatures of habit:

> I have always wanted to write novels in which my heroes would say 'What would happen to me without my hours at the office' or again 'My wife is dead, but happily I have a big stack of orders to write tomorrow'.[2]

To many critics, Meursault seems such an unconscious hero, ignorant of the meaning of his life. Because of this interpretation, they think that Meursault changes too much at the end of the novel, when he becomes highly intelligent and very articulate. Camus is criticised for a break in the novel's style. In *Le Mythe de Sisyphe*, however,

Camus speaks of the possibility of a clerk as an absurd hero equal to those more flamboyant characters he describes:

> The lover, the actor, or the adventurer plays the absurd. But equally well, if he wishes, the chaste man, the civil servant, or the President of the Republic. It is enough to know and to mask nothing.[3]

The central question for an understanding of *L'Etranger* is whether Meursault is an unconscious hero or the absurd hero of *Le Mythe de Sisyphe*. Some recent critics have felt that in his narrative Meursault shows intelligence and sensitivity, and a consistent personal attitude towards moral issues. He is now often accepted as a consciously "absurd man"; and, according to Philip Thody, Camus confirmed this reading in private conversation.[4] Meursault's life is not a clear illustration of Camus's idea of revolt. But, as Camus says in *Le Mythe de Sisyphe*, philosophical novels are not thesis novels; the artist is "convinced of the uselessness of any principle of explanation and sure of the educative message of perceptible appearance."[5]

Meursault, after rejecting his employer's offer of a job in Paris, hints at an earlier experience that shaped his attitude:

> I saw no reason for 'changing my life'. By and large it wasn't an unpleasant one. As a student I'd had plenty of ambition of the kind he meant. But, when I had to drop my studies, I very soon realized all that was pretty futile.[6]

Because he realises that he cannot impose a meaningful pattern on life, Meursault consciously rejects economic and social ambitions. He sees the lack of coherence in the world, and he refuses the usual abstractions that men place between themselves and reality.

What Meursault values is present sensation, concrete experience. His indifference is only to such conventional aims as promotion or marriage. He is far from indifferent to immediate sources of pleasure or displeasure in the external world. His descriptions of natural phenomena show an aesthetic sensitivity and an intelligent power of direct observation; these are essential features of his character. As he realises in prison, the values in his past life were "warm smells of summer, my favourite streets, the sky at evening, Marie's dresses and her laugh."[7] Truth is what he feels, and beyond this he refuses to commit himself. In his narrative, Meursault is scrupulously honest in describing what happens, but he refuses to explain occurrences rationally. He will not generalise from his momentary pleasure with Marie to a permanent emotion called love. He knows no other explanation for his crime except "because of the sun." When his defence counsel pleads with him to say that he is grieved by his mother's death, Meursault refuses; to him "grief" is a meaningless abstraction.

Meursault's relationship with his mother is, however, less simple than at first appears. Some additional light is shed on the relationship of mother and son by secondary episodes in the novel. Raymond and his Arab mistress live in a tense emotional state between love and hatred. A similar ambiguous relationship is described in the story of Salamano, another of Meursault's neighbours. Salamano is a rather pathetic old man, leading a joyless existence centred upon his mangy dog, whom he mistreats. Salamano and the dog seem to distrust and hate each other. Yet, when the dog disappears, Meursault hears Salamano crying during the night. Meursault remarks, with his usual refusal to probe his feelings, "For some reason, I don't know what, I began thinking of Mother."[8] Later, when being questioned by his counsel about his apparent lack of grief at his mother's funeral, Meursault comments:

I could truthfully say I'd been quite fond of Mother—
but really that didn't mean much. All normal people, I
added, as an afterthought, had more or less desired the
death of those they loved, at some time or another.[9]

It is rare indeed, and adds to the intensity of this passage,
that the taciturn Meursault volunteers anything as "an
afterthought."

Indirectly, Camus indicates that Meursault has more
complicated feelings than might appear from his detached
method of narration. Meursault is not a moral monster,
nor is he devoid of normal human sensibilities. His attitude towards his mother, like the attitude of Raymond
towards his mistress, or of Salamano towards his dog, is
an ambiguous mixture of love and hatred. Meursault
recognises this, but because of his desire to speak only of
what he can describe clearly, he limits his statements
about his mother to the exact feelings of particular
moments. He will not assume the stereotyped role of loving
son, even though it might save his life during the trial.

Meursault has opted for the earth, for the immediate
course of events, and for a use of his intelligence only
within those limited areas where he can find certainty.
He is condemned because his way of life is not acceptable
to society. An excellent analysis of his point of view is
contained in Robert Champigny's *Sur un héros païen*, a
study of Meursault as a pagan hero in opposition to a
Christian society. Meursault, as Champigny sees him,
adopts an epicurean moral code. The epicurean begins
with a feeling of innocence and a desire to find happiness.
Happiness consists in not suffering physically or psychi-
cally; one avoids suffering by suppressing non-natural
needs, such as ambition and vanity. More positively, one
seeks pleasure in an harmonious relationship with the
external world. Champigny shows how Meursault's
adaptation to his condition in prison can be called epicurean wisdom. Meursault refuses to suffer; he fills his

time with simple memories and with the concrete experiences that prison offers: the daily walk and the visits of his counsel, whose vari-coloured ties are a diversion in the routine. In order not to disturb his equilibrium, Meursault is even able to suppress his sexual desires.

Fault for an epicurean results from putting oneself out of harmony with the natural world. In contrast, the Christian begins with a feeling of guilt, and seeks, not harmony with the world, but a withdrawal from the world into God. Christianity does not see the natural world as an all-embracing scene but as a divine creation divided into soul and flesh. The Christian feels himself in exile in the natural world, and he tries to follow divinely ordained laws so that he may be favourably judged after death. Champigny's distinction between pagan and Christian is similar to the distinction between Mediterranean and Nordic world views that Camus elaborates in *L'Homme révolté*. Meursault, many of whose traits are based on those of the young Algerians whom Camus describes in *Noces*, is, in some respects, the Mediterranean hero whose moral and metaphysical view of life might be a saving force for European civilisation.

For Meursault morality consists in acting in accordance with his sentiments; he must describe these sentiments, to himself and to other people, honestly and without exaggeration. Society's morality, however, consists in obedience to an *a priori* code, which is held to be of universal validity. Those who accept this code are forced to deny any sentiments that conflict with it; their position is thus precarious. For this reason the person bound by convention sees a refusal to abide by the moral law, or to repent if one has broken it, as an attempt to undermine the sense of his own life. This, as Champigny demonstrates, is the underlying meaning of the amusing and grotesque scene between Meursault and the examining magistrate. Meursault denies any belief in God, but the magistrate cannot accept this:

That was unthinkable, he said; all men believe in God, even those who reject Him. Of this he was absolutely sure; if ever he came to doubt it, his life would lose all meaning. 'Do you wish,' he asked indignantly, 'my life to have no meaning?' Really I couldn't see how my wishes came into it, and I told him as much.[10]

Society's legal judgments have a similar religious base; revenge against those who break the sacred law is behind most systems of punishment. It is evident that the public prosecutor feels Meursault's real crime to be a denial of the moral code by which society attempts to establish stability. Meursault is condemned as much for his refusal to cry at his mother's funeral as for his refusal to repent for the death of the Arab.

Meursault does not regard the killing as a sin. It is an error, caused by the blinding presence of the sun. He feels at fault only because he has disturbed the relationship between himself and the natural world; he has "shattered the balance of the day."[11] After his imprisonment he accepts his legal status as a criminal, but he only gradually realises why society considers his whole mode of life to be guilty. (Although Meursault is conscious of the "absurdity" of life, he is nevertheless quite naïve about social values, and he finds religious perspectives especially difficult to comprehend.) He finally accepts his social role, not by feeling guilt or sin, but by defending his life as the one value he has and by taking a defiant attitude towards the society that has condemned him. He hopes to be greeted with cries of hatred as he goes to the scaffold; having taken on the role of society's "moral monster," he wants to play it to the end. His scorn for the religious system that has condemned him will bear witness to his concept of truth. As he articulates clearly the view of life implicit in all his narrative, Meursault becomes a hero; in Camus's words Meursault is "the only Christ we deserve."[12]

Indeed, Meursault plays a Christ-like role, witnessing to a true relationship between man and the world. Details in his story are meant to recall the life of Christ. Meursault refuses three times to tell the examining magistrate why he fired four shots into the dead body on the beach; later, he refuses three times to see the prison chaplain. These refusals to compromise with society and religion are analogous to Christ's three refusals to be tempted by Satan. Meursault's silence at his trial might be compared to Christ's silence before Pilate. Meursault, like Christ, is condemned not because of his overt actions but because the public believes that he is a social menace. Meursault accepts his role and desires to be executed in front of an angry crowd. His language recalls the Gospel: "For all to be accomplished."[13]

L'Etranger records man's struggle with the external world as well as his conflict with society. The novel is a concrete image of what Camus terms the absurd confrontation between man's desires and the indifference of the universe. Meursault shares the fundamental traits attributed to man in *Le Mythe de Sisyphe*: a desire for life and a desire for truth. He encounters, however, the limitations that the universe places upon his desires. Meursault's simple needs, mostly physical, are often frustrated; he is especially aware of the sun's heat, which frequently saps his energy. The opposition between Meursault and the sun culminates in the murder scene on the beach. The sun becomes blinding and unbearable; it confuses Meursault's senses and crushes his body. He knows that it is "stupid" to walk towards the Arab, but he is not able to resist.

Meursault wants to escape the sun's heat; his act is thus an attempted rebellion against the hostility of the external world. Although we may accept Champigny's suggestion that Meursault is a pagan hero trying to live in harmony with the universe, we must remember that for Camus such harmony is not fully possible. Revolt is in man's nature. Meursault's revolt is not the romantic revolt of Camus's more flamboyant heroes, such as Caligula, but it is a conscious act. Even if his first shot is an unthinking movement, Meursault fires four additional shots into the inert body, thus accepting personal responsibility for his act. (Germaine Brée, who had access to *La Mort heureuse*, an earlier, abandoned novel, similar to *L'Etranger*, finds in it a less ambiguous treatment of revolt against the universe.)[14]

Meursault imprisoned symbolises man caught in a hostile world. He becomes less self-assured, less able to communicate with others. He is a stranger to himself, and he is separated from Marie. (The evil universe in *La Peste* also manifests its power by the separation of loved ones.) His only protest against his imprisonment is his sterile effort to remember and set in order every detail of his room. Like the absurd artist, Meursault tries to repeat and to mime an external reality that he cannot otherwise conquer. He sees himself in prison as a Sisyphus, condemned to a never-ending task:

> To me it seemed like one and the same day that had been going on since I'd been in my cell, and that I'd been doing the same thing all the time.[15]

Details and phrases, especially in the concluding pages of the novel, call to mind Camus's descriptions of the "absurd universe" in *Le Mythe de Sisyphe*. They suggest that Meursault's real enemy is not the *bourgeois* society of Algiers but the inevitable force of death in the universe. Meursault realises that his execution is the fate awaiting all men.

Although he becomes an enemy of human society, Meursault attains a harmony with the universe that has condemned him. He arrives at a point from which he can look back on his life as a completed entity. He accepts his life as a value in itself; in accepting this value he accepts his death. He feels himself opening to the "benign indifference of the universe."[16] Champigny suggests that this is similar to the stage in epicurean philosophy where fear of death is conquered. A Freudian interpretation might be that Meursault returns to the harmony with nature that only animals feel. As Norman Brown in a recent study of Freudian thought explains:

> Lower organisms live the life proper to their species; their individuality consists in their being concrete embodiments of the essence of their species in a particular life which ends in death.[17]

Man represses his bodily nature and thus fears death:

> Repression generates the instinctual compulsion to change the internal nature of man and the external world in which he lives, thus giving man a history and subordinating the life of the individual to the historical quest of the species.[18]

Man could attain true happiness and individuality only by giving up his impossible compulsion to change the world and to avoid death. Meursault, on the eve of his execution, accepts death as the culmination of his own individuality. He reaches that peace of which Camus sometimes speaks, a point at which the tension of the rebel is no longer felt, "a tranquil homeland where death itself is a happy silence."[19] This homeland is beyond the grasp of a man who is in revolt against the universe, a man who is involved in the history of his species. It may seem paradoxical to find a quest for such peace at the heart of Camus's work, but in an ultimate sense Camus's experience confirms Freud's insight. Accepting the natural world as the source of all happiness necessitates accepting death. Man rebels, but he reaches a final consent. This is not a betrayal of his desires, but an affirmation of his greatness when he no longer attempts to be a god.

Meursault's acceptance of simple, spontaneous happiness in the physical world and his moral preoccupation with a just and unexaggerated use of language are values with which Camus is in agreement: simple values that may be a step beyond nihilism. *L'Etranger* is, however, an ironic novel. Camus insists that a novelist should not preach; he should treat his fundamental concerns comically and lightly, holding them at a distance. Because of the irony and humour with which the story is told, we cannot read *L'Etranger* as a simple allegorical representation of man against the universe. The universe is the ultimate force against which Meursault revolts, and which crushes him, but this force acts through a social order that is comically portrayed. The examining magistrate and the public prosecutor are both grotesque caricatures of commonly accepted religious and social attitudes. Their interpretation of Meursault's behaviour is patently ridiculous: "I accuse the prisoner of behaving at his mother's funeral in a way that showed he was already a criminal at heart."[20] The trial is a parody of judicial process, and the verdict is hardly a clear-cut symbol of universal human mortality. As Meursault comments:

The fact that the verdict was read out at 8 p.m. rather than at 5, the fact that it might have been quite different, that it was given by men who change their underclothes, and was credited to so vague an entity as the 'French People'—for that matter, why not to the Chinese or the German People?—all these facts seemed to deprive the court's decision of much of its gravity.[21]

Although Meursault becomes articulate in the final pages of his narrative, throughout his life he is a very unassuming hero. His boredom at certain times, especially during the Sunday he spends on his balcony, is almost antithetical to the passionate interest in every moment that Camus describes in *Le Mythe de Sisyphe*. The desires that place Meursault in opposition to the universe are only simple preferences for *café au lait*, clean washroom towels, and a chance to smoke in prison. Meursault's companions, whose names seem to prefigure his Christ-like martyrdom, are an amiable but rather pathetic Céleste, an Emmanuel too stupid to follow the plot sat the cinema, and an easy-going, non-spiritual Marie. Since he has murdered someone, Meursault is a paradoxical representative of man's desire for life. This is perhaps the most ironic twist in the story; it negates any simple reading of Meursault as a "hero of the absurd." Cyril Connolly suggests that the neglect of Meursault's victim is "a failure of sensibility on the part of Camus."[22] Meursault is not indeed concerned for his victim, but Camus deliberately created a hero with limitations. He draws attention to this irony in *La Peste*; Cottard, a reprehensible criminal who is happy during the plague, is frightened by the story of Meursault's crime because it reminds him of his own past.[23]

Although Meursault wants to be a martyr, his martyrdom will have no practical value. In one of the first mentions of the theme of *L'Etranger* in his notebooks, Camus remarks on the ironic character of the story as he first conceived it:

> The man does not want to justify himself. The idea that is made up about him is preferred to the man himself. He dies, alone in being conscious of his truth. Vanity of this consolation.[24]

Like irony, artistic form creates an essential distance between the author's experience and the completed work. The contrived narrative form of *L'Etranger* keeps the reader at a distance from the story and reminds him that it is fiction. Meursault begins his story: "Mother died today." We assume that we are either reading a diary or following an interior monologue. Within a page, however, Meursault speaks of another day, with no indication of transition. The second chapter begins on a "today" which is Saturday and ends on Sunday. Since in this chapter he has gone to bed with Marie on Saturday night, without any chance to record his day, Meursault cannot be writing a diary. But *L'Etranger* is not an interior monologue, because Meursault describes events in a past tense. This confusion is compounded by occasional remarks which suggest that Meursault is writing a retrospective account:

> I even had an impression that the dead body in their midst meant nothing at all to them. But now I suspect that I was mistaken about this.[25]

It seems logically impossible to understand how Meursault can write or tell his story. Perhaps the most ingenious explanation for Camus's confusing use of time in the novel is Champigny's. Meursault, he says, is writing his story at the end of his life, when he has accepted his destiny. The narrative is another way, in addition to the martyr's role he intends to play at his execution, of witnessing to the truth of his life. However, because Meursault sees this truth as a product of immediate sensations, he tries to recapture his feelings at various moments, and he is aided in doing so by recounting events as if they had just happened. This explanation also takes into account how Meursault can represent himself as naïve at the trial, and yet can show, by many ironic touches, that he now understands why he was thrust into the role of a social "monster." Yet Champigny admits that the idea of Meursault writing in this manner is not probable. We are left with a realisation that the novel is an artificial pattern imposed upon an experience.

When *L'Etranger* is examined more closely, there are many signs of this artificial pattern. Sartre, in his essay on *L'Etranger*, comments on the form, which resembles that of the eighteenth-century moralists, and which contrasts with the theme of a disordered world: "*L'Etranger* is a classical work, a work of order composed about the absurd and against the absurd."[26] The novel is divided into two parts, the first part describing Meursault's life until the murder and the second describing his imprisonment and trial. The two-part structure provides a set of contrasts between two ways of looking at the world. The two parts contrast Meursault's acceptance of immediate sensations as truth with society's need to find abstract motivations. Each of the events that Meursault describes in his objective manner in Part One—his mother's funeral, his affair with Marie, his attempt to help Raymond—is seen in a totally different light during the trial. We have, as Sartre remarks, "on the one hand, the amorphous, everyday flow of reality . . . and on the other the edifying reconstruction of this reality by human reason."[27]

The two parts of the novel also show the two faces of the external world. When he is free, Meursault is able to enjoy the beauty of nature, physical contact with Marie, simple companionship with others. When imprisoned, Meursault is placed in a cell where he cannot see the external world; his contact with Marie is reduced to a sterile interview in the prison visiting room; his attempts to be friendly with his counsel are rebuffed. This duality is also shown by the variation in Meursault's feeling of time. When he is free, Meursault sees every moment as valuable in itself; each event is described as occurring at a precise time. In prison, all days seem monotonous; he summarises eleven months in a few pages.

The language of the novel is also carefully patterned, showing a similar variation in each of the two sections. In accordance with his distrust of abstraction, Meursault's normal style of writing is extremely matter-of-fact. His sentences are short descriptions of precise events; his vocabulary is restricted and concrete. He gives everything equal weight; he does not establish connexions between events in terms of any rational causality. When he is emotionally aroused, his style and tone subtly change. He occasionally writes brief poetic passages describing some landscape that gives him a sense of beauty or of peace.

At the end of each part of the novel, there is a violent break in the normal tone. When Meursault goes to the beach to meet the Arab, his language becomes highly metaphorical. He feels the sun as a personal force, an opponent from whom he must escape; he describes this hostile sun with many striking personifications. As well as depicting Meursault's state of mind, the emotional tone of this passage creates a sense of something more mysterious, more dreadful than the murder of a nameless Arab. We feel the metaphysical nature of Meursault's act as a protest against the universe. After his outburst against the prison chaplain, Meursault reaches another heightened state. This is the final realisation that "all is well," a feeling of peace with the universe. Again Meursault's language attains a poetic level. The balanced two-part structure, with parallel events and parallel tonal patterns, is part of the classical order, as Camus understands it, that the artist must impose on his material.

The plot of *L'Etranger* is built around death and judgment. From the first page, a feeling of judgment against Meursault is gradually built up. He feels vaguely at fault, even when asking his employer's permission to attend his mother's funeral. In his interview with the director of the old people's home, he states: "I had a feeling he was blaming me for something."[28] At the vigil before the funeral, the old people look at Meursault curiously: "For a moment I had an absurd impression that they had come to sit in judgment on me."[29] After the murder, Meursault sees himself as a criminal. He is frightened by the examining magistrate, but reminds himself, "it was absurd to feel like this, considering that, after all, it was I who was the criminal."[30] Still later, Meursault realises that his way of life and not only his crime is being judged, that he is guilty in the eyes of society.

These scenes of judgment and death are inter-connected by repeated images of intense light. The vigil scene is flooded by a blinding, artificial light; the sun blinds Meursault on the beach before he shoots. (Earlier, when Raymond handed him the revolver, the sun glinted on it.) Meursault is disturbed by the heat and the light in the magistrate's chambers, and later in the courtroom, where the prosecutor announces he will prove Meursault's guilt "by the facts of the crime, which are as clear as daylight."[31] These images of light and heat are balanced by images of coolness, evening, and the sea, images that are frequently associated with Marie or with Meursault's mother. Meursault meets Marie in the water; when she comes to visit him in prison, he is looking at the sea; while watching the cool evening sky after his acceptance of death, he thinks of her and of his mother.

In *Noces* Camus speaks of the Algerian people as "a whole race born of the sun and the sea."[32] The sea is often a feminine principle in Camus's universe; the sun is dominant and masculine. Sun and sea, masculine and feminine, are identified with the two opposing faces of the world: hostility and beauty. Meursault revolts against the sun, against the hostile masculinity of the world. During the trial, the public prosecutor compares Meursault's crime with that of a parricide who is next on the court's agenda; neither criminal has accepted society's moral code. Although his perspective is wrong, the prosecutor is, ironically, correct in his association. Meursault's crime is directed against the universal father and oppressor, the sun. Meursault's final state of peace, when he understands his mother and accepts his approaching death, is a reconciliation with the universe as a feminine source of beauty. Through the sun and sea imagery of the novel, Camus suggests that Meursault's act may be considered as a murder of the father in order to reach harmony with the mother.

Camus uses indirect methods to suggest the deeper layers of meaning in *L'Etranger*. The secondary incidents reflect on the ambiguity of Meursault's feelings for his mother. The imagery reinforces the symbolic theme of a revolt against the universe, and it suggests the archetypal sexual nature of this revolt. The parallels to the life of Christ add to our understanding of Meursault as the hero in opposition to his society. A view of the world and of human nature is implied beneath the surface of the story, but no clear didactic message emerges. Meursault, "the only Christ we deserve," is a comic saviour, created to mock the universe.

REFERENCES

1. *E.*, p. 64 (49).
2. *E.E.*, p. 109.
3. *M.S.*, p. 124 (75).
4. Philip Thody, *Albert Camus: 1913–1960* (1961), p. 37.
5. *M.S.*, p. 138 (83).
6. *E.*, p. 64 (49).
7. *E.*, p. 148 (110).
8. *E.*, p. 61 (48).
9. *E.*, p. 94 (71).
10. *E.*, p. 99 (75).
11. *E.*, p. 88 (67–8).
12. Preface to *L'Etranger*, p. 548.
13. *E.*, p. 172 (127).
14. Germaine Brée, *Camus* (1959), pp. 64–7.
15. *E.*, p. 115 (86–7).
16. *E.*, pp. 171–2 (127).
17. Norman Brown, *Life Against Death* (1959), p. 105.
18. *Op. cit.*, p. 105.
19. *E.E.*, p. 33.
20. *E.*, p. 137 (102).
21. *E.*, p. 154 (114).
22. Cyril Connolly, Introduction to *The Outsider* (1946), p. 10.
23. *P.*, p. 68 (55).
24. *Carnets*, p. 46.
25. *E.*, p. 20 (20).
26. Sartre, *Situations I* (1947), p. 121.
27. *Op. cit.*, p. 110.
28. *E.*, p. 11 (12).
29. *E.*, p. 19 (18).
30. *E.*, p. 99 (75).
31. *E.*, p. 140 (104).
32. *N.*, p. 26.

CHAPTER V

LA PESTE

La Peste (1947) is a novel dealing with an epidemic of plague that supposedly struck Oran sometime in the nineteen-forties. The story is told in the third-person by Dr Rieux, who does not identify himself as the narrator until the final pages. Although he is a prominent figure in the action that he relates, Rieux tries to maintain an objective attitude towards it.

Rieux begins his narrative with a description of Oran before the plague struck. He sees his fellow citizens caught in routine, incapable of moving beyond their daily quest for money:

> Certainly nothing is commoner nowadays than to see people working from morn till night and then proceeding to fritter away at card-tables, in cafés and in small talk what time is left for living. Nevertheless, there still exist towns and countries where people have now and again an inkling of something different. In general it doesn't change their lives. Still, they have had an intimation, and that's so much to the good. Oran, however, seems to be a town without intimations, in other words, completely modern.[1]

The physical appearance of Oran contributes to the citizens' complacency. The bay and the mountains are beautiful, but Oran has been constructed as a walled town, with its back to the sea. Its buildings are singularly ugly and dusty. Oran is a town without trees, without glamour, and without a soul. In such an atmosphere it is easy to become numb and to forget the rebellious desires that place men in opposition to the world. The people of Oran, as Rieux describes them, are incapable of recognising that a hostile universe might disturb their secure routine.

Rieux's first hint of something extraordinary is his discovery of a dead rat on his doorstep. The rats, carriers of the bubonic plague, come out of their holes to die. Like others in the community, Rieux at first ignores this strange phenomenon. He is preoccupied with his wife, who is ill and about to leave the city for a rest cure in the mountains. Rieux feels guilty; because of his medical duties, he has neglected his wife. Concerned only with personal problems, he is at first incapable of understanding that the rats foretell a threat to his security.

The rats die in increasing numbers; then men begin to die. City officials are slow to admit that there is a plague for them to deal with, but when the death-rate has risen sufficiently, they are forced to declare a state of contagion and seal off the city from the outside world. Within the closed city of Oran, the plague takes a vast toll of lives, in spite of the efforts of doctors and volunteer workers to fight it. After nine months, the plague's force decreases and the city is freed from its terror; the community returns to normal life. Those who fought the plague do not know whether they have won a victory or merely benefited from chance. Meditating on what he has learned from his experience, Rieux decides that the struggle for life is worth while. He knows, however, that the plague may return, that it can never be defeated.

Camus terms *La Peste* a chronicle rather than a novel. He draws upon Defoe's *Journal of the Plague Year* for many incidents, and for the general pattern of life during the epidemic. But Camus's account is drier and less dramatic than Defoe's. The story reproduces a feeling of the monotony and routine of life in Oran. There is no plot-structure beyond a cycle of normality—plague—return to normality. *La Peste* recounts a struggle between the

epidemic and the community. Those individuals who
stand out in the community are treated episodically,
appearing from time to time on a stage that is dominated
by a destructive force and a suffering body of men. Camus
divides the book into five sections of varying lengths, each
covering one phase in the history of the plague. This five-
part construction is used to emphasise the relative unim-
portance of individuals within the struggle. The first and
final parts describe the city before and after the plague,
at times when dates can be mentioned and when personal
activities have importance. The second and fourth sections of the novel contain fewer references to precise
events and to individuals; they describe the sufferings
and activities of the whole population. The short centre
section portrays the community at the height of the
epidemic. Time seems to have stopped, and individuals
have lost their personal characteristics. They are reduced
by the plague to a less than human state in which even
suffering and despair have become routine.

The people of Oran and the plague, which seems to
have a personality of its own, are the principal characters
of the novel. There are, as well, a small group of men
with whom Rieux is in contact, and who react in various
ways to the coming of the epidemic. At one end of the
scale of reactions is an old asthma patient whose life
seems completely untouched by the plague. He is a
strange "absurd" hero. As he believes that life has no
meaning, he decides that the best way to live is to do as
little as possible. He spends his days in bed, transferring
dried peas from one pot to another, a mechanical activity
which incidentally tells him when it is time to eat. The
appearance of the rats gives this old man a strange joy;
and at those times when the plague causes most deaths in
the city his health improves. He seems to be an enemy of
man, a supporter of the plague. His way of life is the
opposite of that of Dr Rieux, who spends his days giving
vaccinations, caring for suffering patients, and making

arrangements to bury the victims of the plague. Yet the old man appears to understand the nature of life more clearly than many of the active heroes; it is impossible to judge him unfavourably. He represents, in the total framework of the novel, an element of irony, which shows the limitations of heroic action.

It is, in fact, difficult to prove that the activities of those who fight the plague are efficacious. Perhaps they alleviate the suffering of the victims; perhaps the system of isolating a family when one member has been stricken keeps the death-toll lower. The fight against the plague has limited value, but it teaches something of the nature of life. The other characters are forced by the plague to re-examine their values, to consider their experience in a new light. They learn what the old asthma patient has always known: "But what does that mean—'plague'? Just life, no more than that."[2] The novel makes it clear that the educational value of the plague does not justify the suffering endured. As Camus remarks in his notebooks for *La Peste*, the plague brings the benefit of forcing one to think, but, considering the misery it produces, one would be mad or criminal to consent to it.[3]

Camus includes among his characters Cottard, a criminal wanted by the police. Before the plague struck, Cottard had attempted to commit suicide, but now he finds that everyone is in the same boat, everyone is hunted. Cottard is happier because the epidemic makes him feel part of the group. As another character remarks of him:

> His only real crime is that of having in his heart approved of something that killed off men, women and children. I can understand the rest, but for *that* I am obliged to pardon him.[4]

As the plague ends, Cottard is again sought by the police. He goes mad, barricades himself in his room, and fires a gun into the street. The only creature he kills, however, is a dog; his crime is his moral attitude rather than any overt act.

Although it is not spectacular, Rieux's moral growth is subtly delineated during the course of the action. Rieux begins his account with an ironic portrait of the normal life of Oran. He is aloof from his fellow men; while telling his story he detaches himself from the community. His attitude alternates between sympathy towards others and an ironic judgment of them. This shift is subtly indicated in Rieux's language; he refers to the suffering men of Oran as "we," but he describes the foolish behaviour of "our fellow citizens." Rieux is torn between his desire to speak for everyone, to see himself as part of the community, and his natural feelings of condescension and aloofness. Through fighting the plague he learns that, in spite of their foolishness and their ignorance, men are more to be admired than despised. Watching the celebrations after the opening of the city gates, Rieux looks down from a balcony on the joyful crowd and sympathises with them.

Besides greater respect for his fellow men, Rieux gains a clearer understanding of the permanent and meaningless evil in the world. Before the plague begins, Rieux describes himself as tired of this world in which there is so much suffering. As he fights the plague and sees that his medical efforts are of little use, he loses his few illusions about his ability as a doctor and about the permanence of love and friendship. His wife dies in the sanatorium, and the closest of his friends, Tarrou, is killed by the plague. Rieux has only the lucid but hopeless knowledge of the world that Meursault attained in prison:

But what had he, Rieux, won? No more than the experience of having known plague and remembering it, of having known friendship and remembering it, of knowing affection and being destined one day to remember it. So all a man could win in the conflict between plague and life was knowledge and memories.

But Rieux adds, "Tarrou, perhaps, would have called that winning the match."[5]

Tarrou organises teams of men to help the doctors inoculate and isolate patients. He fights the plague because he is obsessed with death and with the necessity to combat it. Shortly before his death, he tells Rieux his life story. (Tarrou's early life bears a striking similarity to that of the hero of Robert Louis Stevenson's *Weir of Hermiston*. Camus often draws upon a wide range of literary sources, and he boldly enriches his own work by an implied criticism of other responses to life's "absurdity.") Tarrou awakened to absurdity when he was seventeen. Tarrou's father, a public prosecutor, invited his young son to hear him plead a murder case. Rather than being impressed by his father's oratorical skill, the boy felt a strange identification with the poor, bewildered criminal. "I only knew that they were set on killing that living man and an uprush of some elemental instinct, like a wave, had swept me to his side."[6] Aware that life has intrinsic value in itself and that society denies this value, Tarrou left home and became a political revolutionary. When he realises that revolutions also use violence, that he too has condoned some form of murder, Tarrou is left defenceless. All men, he feels, carry within themselves the germ of the plague, a desire for violence; the most he can do is to limit the damage by fighting for the victims. The plague in Oran gives him an opportunity for purer action than he could find in any political situation.

Tarrou conscientiously develops an ironic awareness of life's absurdity. He keeps notebooks, jotting down all the meaningless activity about him. He takes a strange delight in the ugliness of Oran, finding in the sordid commercial character of the city a confirmation of his view of life. These notebooks, which Rieux incorporates into his narrative, also describe Tarrou's attempts to find inner peace, to kill the germ of the plague within himself. He is obsessed with a desire to understand yet not to pass judgment. It is Tarrou who tries to befriend Cottard, the criminal. Tarrou defines his search as an attempt to be a saint without God, to reach what seems an impossible purity of thought and action.

Tarrou remains a strange and lonely figure, but he tries to understand others. Rieux overcomes some of his natural distrust of his fellows. The other characters also learn a measure of human solidarity. Paneloux, a Jesuit priest, preaches that the epidemic is God's vengeance for sins. As he watches innocent children dying, he changes his views. In a second sermon he identifies himself with the community, whose suffering, as he now realises, is not caused by moral shortcomings. Death and suffering are incomprehensible, but Paneloux must retain his faith in God. He adopts a Kierkegaardian Christianity. If God is neither just nor good, as man can understand Him, man must make a leap of faith. He must will the absurd human condition because God wills it. Paneloux (whose name suggests a praise of all things) accepts everything, even irrationality and death, as part of God's will. He helps to alleviate the suffering of others, but finds an austere strength to accept suffering for himself. He dies of the plague after refusing to call a doctor.

Raymond Rambert, a Parisian journalist caught in Oran when the gates close, also finds a role in the community. After many attempts to escape from the city to rejoin the woman he loves, he realises that he could not be happy while others suffer. He is not a stranger in Oran; he must stay, work, and suffer with the community. Even the least sympathetic character in the novel, Judge Othon, undergoes a conversion after the death of his young son. He loses some of his uncompromising rigidity, his respect for law and order. Rather than return to the bench as a judge, he wants to administer a camp for those quarantined in the plague.

It is easy to read *La Peste* as a story of heroism and pure moral intentions, but to do so would be to find a simple thesis that Camus does not intend. We must not overlook the irony; the limitations of the heroes are subtly indicated in the novel. Such a stiff and uncompromising figure as Judge Othon cannot become an exemplary hero. Father Paneloux shows moral courage, but his acceptance of the absurd is a form of philosophical suicide. Less evident, but more important, is the irony in the presentation of the three figures who share many of Camus's moral attitudes: Rambert, Tarrou, and Rieux.

Rambert is described very sympathetically. He is a more human, less dedicated figure than Tarrou or Rieux; the reader sympathises with his fight for personal happiness. His attempt to escape from Oran—one of the few dramatic incidents in a book that aims at reproducing the desperate monotony of living through a plague—is the most rebellious action he can undertake. One of the evils of the plague is its ability to make men seem abstract and less than human. As Rieux complains after he refuses to help Rambert to escape: "To fight abstraction you must have something of it in your own make-up. But how could Rambert be expected to grasp that?"[7] Rambert does not get caught in the abstraction of the plague; when the others have lost even their sense of the passage of time, he counts the days that he has been separated from his mistress. In trying to escape, Rambert upholds the right of men to avoid succumbing to the plague's depersonalising effects.

While Rambert's decision to stay in Oran shows courage, it is perhaps the wrong choice. Since Rieux, whose work as a doctor is more useful than Rambert's, doubts the value of his effort, we wonder whether Rambert's sacrifice is worth while. The novel offers no clear-cut justification for Rambert's action. As Rieux comments:

For nothing in the world is it worth turning one's back

on what one loves. Yet that is what I'm doing—though *why* I do not know.[8]

If Camus approves of Rambert's decision to be part of the community, he realises that such a choice is only partially valid. There is a suggestion in the closing pages of the novel, when Rambert is reunited with his mistress, that he has perhaps sacrificed too much:

he had changed too greatly. The plague had forced on him a detachment which, try as he might, he couldn't think away and which like a formless fear haunted his mind.[9]

Every moral choice in an absurd world is ambiguous, including Tarrou's attempt to be a saint without God. Tarrou seeks a purity of thought and action that is beyond man's ability. It is ironic that, when he explains to Rieux his desire to avoid all violence, two shots are heard at the city gates; the local authorities with whom Tarrou co-operates must use violence against those trying to escape the quarantined city.[10] Tarrou's search for inner peace is noble, but it seems a leap beyond man's situation into the transcendental:

But for those others, who aspired beyond and above the human individual towards something they could not even imagine, there had been no answer. Tarrou might seem to have won through to that hardly-come-by peace of which he used to speak; but he had found it only in death, too late to turn it to account.[11]

Tarrou tries to be a saint, while Rieux is content merely to be a man. This choice meets with Camus's approval, but Rieux too has limitations. Rieux is human, and less than an exemplary hero. Rambert insists on the importance of happiness; he serves as a corrective to Rieux's self-sacrificial stoicism. There is also a discrepancy between Rieux's general principle of serving humanity and his aloof attitude towards many of his fellow men.

He says he is writing "with good feelings,"[12] but his comments are often ironic. Rieux believes in the importance of clear, objective language, but he is sometimes so condescending towards others that he obscures truth from them. The discrepancy between principles and behaviour can be seen in an incident immediately after Rieux has decided that the epidemic is the plague. He is talking with one of his patients, Joseph Grand:

"Well," he said, "perhaps we'd better make up our minds to call this disease by its name. So far we've been only shilly-shallying. . . ."

"Quite so, quite so," said Grand . . . "I too believe in calling things by their name. . . . But what's the name in this case?"

"That I shan't say; and anyhow you wouldn't gain anything by knowing."[13]

Rieux denies that his work is heroic; it is rather a common-sense choice to follow his profession and to meet an obvious need. Rieux proposes, as the real "hero" of his narrative, Joseph Grand. Grand is a small, insignificant man who works as an underpaid clerk in a government office. His wife left him many years before, and he suffers from loneliness and unrequited love. Grand is a hero because he acts on good feelings; he works with Rieux during the plague, not from any intellectual convictions, but simply because he feels that people must help each other.

Although he has given up the search for personal happiness, Rieux feels that this search is more important than brave deeds. Grand is a hero because he manages to keep his personal life intact throughout the long epidemic. His one aim in life is to write a perfect novel, but he has written only its opening sentence, which he keeps varying and improving over many months. In its latest version it reads: "One fine morning in May, a slim young horsewoman might have been seen riding a glossy sorrel mare

F

along the avenues of the Bois, amongst the flowers.''[14] Grand's sentence is his ridiculous but significant protest against the plague; he fights the plague, but he is not dominated by its dehumanising power. Although he seems only a silly old man, Grand is, ironically, the most admirable character in the novel.

The plague represents the power of death and destruction in the universe. It makes such grandiose gestures as inflicting terrible pain on the innocent son of Judge Othon; less dramatically, it forces men to live in a monotonous and routine world, where they must struggle to stay alive, and where their desires for love and pleasure are often thwarted. Life in Oran during the plague, by implication all life, keeps men below the level of their finest sentiments and desires. As Tarrou remarks after seeing the disheartened men in one of the isolation camps:

> they're forgotten, and they know it . . . those they love have forgotten them because all their energies are devoted to making schemes and taking steps to get them out of the camp. And by dint of always thinking about these schemes and steps they have ceased thinking about those whose release they're trying to secure. And that, too, is natural enough. In fact, it comes to this: nobody is capable of really thinking about anyone, even in the worst calamity. For really to think about someone means thinking about that person every minute of the day, without letting one's thoughts be diverted by anything; by meals, by a fly that settles on one's cheek, by household duties, or by a sudden itch somewhere. But there are always flies and itches. That's why life is difficult to live.[15]

Life during the plague is a series of monotonous actions; people queue for food, traffic turns in circles. Even those who fight the plague must submit to its routine. They must develop an indifference to suffering; they must forego the very sympathy, happiness, and love for which they are fighting. The plague forces its opponents to descend to its inhuman level. The plague also symbolises the incomprehensibility of the universe; it comes and goes unexpectedly. Seeming victories against it may be pure chance. Rieux remarks when the death-rate begins to decline:

Really, however, it is doubtful if this could be called a victory. All that could be said was that the disease seemed to be leaving as unaccountably as it had come.[16]

The plague is not an exceptional phenomenon but the condition in which we live. This universality is suggested by the sun and sea imagery of *La Peste*, which has reson- ances similar to those in *L'Etranger*. The sun is often equated with the force of the plague, whose intensity coincides with the hottest days of summer:

The sun stalked our townsfolk along every byway, into every nook, and when they paused it struck. Since this first onslaught of the heat synchronized with a startling increase in the number of victims—there were now nearly seven hundred deaths a week—a profound dis- couragement settled on the town . . . every door was shut, nobody was to be seen, even the venetian blinds stayed down, and there was no knowing if it was the heat or the plague that they were trying to shut out.[17]

Scenes of death and suffering take place in a hot, often stifling, atmosphere.

The sea is a symbol of nature as a source of beauty; it provides escape from the hostile heat of the sun. During the plague, the city gates are closed and bathing in the sea is forbidden; all contact with the world is reduced to the deadly touch of the plague's heat. The sea is only a promise for the future. Rambert looks towards the sea while thinking of his mistress. Rieux and Tarrou leave the city for a brief swim. They achieve a sense of physical harmony with the universe; they escape, temporarily, from the plague's domination. But they must return to the fight.

The plague is not only a symbol of the irrationality that governs life, it is also symbolic of the oppression suffered by the French people during the German Occupation. In December 1942, Camus noted:

> I want to express by means of the plague, the suffocation from which we have all suffered, and the atmosphere of menace and exile in which we have lived. I want at the same time to extend this interpretation to the notion of existence generally.[18]

Details about life in Oran during the epidemic often recall life in occupied France. The men who fight the plague resemble those with whom Camus worked in "Combat." Father Paneloux is given an heroic role, because Camus wants to render homage to those Christians (such as his close friend, René Leynaud, who was captured and executed by the Germans) who sacrificed themselves in the Resistance movement.[19] The social organisation in Oran resembles that in occupied countries during the War; victims and their families are isolated in special camps, a curfew is imposed, communications with the outside world are suspended. People are initially lulled into a false sense of security similar to that of the Phoney War. The end of the plague is marked by two celebrations: the first when the death rate declines, the second when the city gates are reopened. A parallel to the liberation of Paris and the end of the War in Europe is suggested.

The parallel between war and plague is not always, however, clear-cut. There are some details in *La Peste* that are more applicable to the War than to the plague. The cinemas and theatres remain open, in spite of the obvious dangers of contagion. Shortages of food, petrol, and clothing are an acute problem in Oran. This suggests war-time France rather than a plague in any modern city, where incoming supplies would presumably be more adequate. Since the plague lasts fewer than ten months, incongruity is especially evident when Camus mentions that worn clothing reflects Oran's exile from the outside world. Camus speaks of the separation of families and of lovers as one of the most harmful and discouraging effects of the plague; this also seems more applicable to life in a divided France than to life during an epidemic. Other suggested parallels to the War prove to be ambiguous. The quarantine camps and the incinerators used for cremation, for example, call to mind German concentration camps. Yet, Rieux, who resembles a Resistance hero, is instrumental in setting up the camps and recruiting people to staff them.

These incongruities point to a basic ambiguity: the choice of a natural evil to symbolise a social evil. Since it never necessitates violence against other men, Rieux's work differs from that of the Resistance movement. The people of Oran are innocent victims of the plague; their situation has none of the moral ambiguities of war. Nor are there any characters who resemble those in the Vichy Government. Even Cottard, the criminal, who may seem to symbolise the collaborator, does nothing directly to aid the plague. He is responsible only for the death of a dog.

Many critics feel that the choice of a natural disaster to symbolise war and torture perpetrated by human beings reflects a fundamental weakness in Camus's thought: a disregard of man's guilt. The refusal to consider man's violence is, however, deliberate and ironic. The choice of a plague to represent the hostile forces that man himself can release is similar to the choice of Meursault the murderer to represent innocent humanity in *L'Etranger*. In both novels there is a confusion of issues, which prevents any elementary moral. This ambiguity casts an ironic light on the theme of the novel. The implied parallel to the War shows the limitations of Rieux's belief that men are essentially innocent and admirable.

If the plague is a symbol of human mortality, it is an enemy that can never be defeated. The parallel to the French Resistance suggests, however, that man is fighting a particular enemy that can be conquered. The interplay between a hopeless situation and a situation in which limited victories are possible creates additional ambiguity. If the plague is man's permanent condition, it is ironic to describe this condition as a sporadic phenomenon, which man can help to defeat. When we consider the plague in universal terms, we find that man's heroic action against it has limited value. No activity can change the reality with which man is confronted. All that the heroes of La Peste can accomplish is to increase their own consciousness of absurdity. They uphold man's dignity, but in a hopeless struggle. The fundamental pessimism of the book is somewhat obscured, however, by allusions to the Resistance movement. By making the novel an allegory of war and of the universal fate of man Camus suggests that there are areas in which rebellion can work, but he offers no hope of conclusive victory. Because the plague is not a clear symbol for war or for the hostile universe, indirectness and ambiguity are created. In La Peste, as in L'Etranger, Camus protests against a tragic reality by falsifying and stylising it.

Camus describes man's fate in La Peste with order and restraint. The novel is tightly organised; almost every detail has resonances on several levels. Events and characters reflect on each other, adding nuances of meaning. But the illusion of reading an account of actual occurrences in the city of Oran is not sacrificed to the various symbolic interpretations.

The form and style of the novel exist on two levels: the level at which Rieux writes his "chronicle" as objectively as possible and the level at which Camus creates a myth about man's fate. Rieux often speaks of his narrative method. He tries to be objective: to use clear, precise language, and to describe only the facts. His personal opinions are qualified by such phrases as "it seemed likely," "it was probable." He wants to record the common experiences of the people:

> To be an honest witness, it was for him to confine himself mainly to what people did or said and what could be gleaned from documents. Regarding his personal troubles and his long suspense, his duty was to hold his peace.[20]

Rieux's style is often awkward; he is interested in a truthful description of what happened, not in artistic effects. His objective attitude breaks down only when he describes events that have great emotional impact on him: the death of an innocent child, his swim with Tarrou, his helpless vigil as he watches Tarrou die. Like Meursault, Rieux resorts to metaphoric language when he is faced with those ultimate questions of life and death that he cannot comprehend rationally.

La Peste is more than Rieux's objective report of happenings in Oran. The language has symbolic implications of which he is unaware. Details are chosen to reflect symbolic meanings or to reinforce the themes. Even the music played in Oran during the plague deals with the separation of lovers. Rambert's one gramophone record is "St James Infirmary." The travelling opera company, forced to stay in Oran when the gates are closed, gives repeated performances of *Orpheus and Eurydice*.

The events are arranged in a careful pattern, based on the five parts into which Camus divides the novel. Parts I and V and Parts II and IV contain many parallel episodes. The five sections of the novel suggest a circle of experience, from the commonplace to the height of suffering and then returning to ordinary life. This circle will begin again, for the plague bacillus never dies. The arrangement of the novel suggests that man's history is a cyclical repetition. This is similar to what Camus describes in *L'Homme révolté* as the Greek view of history, which he contrasts with the eschatological theory of Christianity and Marxism.

There is a great discrepancy between Rieux's statement that he "has made hardly any changes for the sake of artistic effect, except those elementary adjustments needed to present his narrative in a more or less coherent form"[21] and the tightly organised pattern of plot and detail of Camus's novel. This discrepancy between different types of narration creates an ironic effect similar to that produced by the lack of verisimilitude in *L'Etranger*. The reader accepts the conventions of the fiction and reacts within its terms, but he is also aware that it is a fiction: an artistic mockery of reality. *La Peste* shows a tension between faithfully describing the world and protesting against it through form and style. Camus describes this tension, in *L'Homme révolté*, as the basis of the novelist's art.

REFERENCES

1. *P.*, p. 14 (6).
2. *P.*, p. 330 (283).
3. "Pages de carnets," p. 4.
4. *P.*, p. 325 (279).
5. *P.*, p. 313 (268).
6. *P.*, p. 269 (230).
7. *P.*, p. 106 (87).
8. *P.*, p. 228 (194).
9. *P.*, p. 316 (271).
10. *P.*, p. 276 (236). See L. R. Rossi, "Albert Camus: The Plague of Absurdity" (1958), p. 421.
11. *P.*, p. 323 (276–7).
12. *P.*, p. 154 (132).
13. *P.*, p. 54 (42).
14. *P.*, p. 284 (245).
15. *P.*, pp. 261–2 (224).
16. *P.*, p. 291 (248–9).
17. *P.*, p. 127 (108).
18. "Pages de carnets," p. 6.
19. See *Actuelles*, p. 247.
20. *P.*, p. 325 (278).
21. *P.*, p. 198 (168).

CHAPTER VI

LA CHUTE

Jean-Baptiste Clamence is the hero of *La Chute* (1956), Camus's third novel. Clamence is a successful Parisian attorney who has given up his career to live in the Amsterdam underworld, where he <u>defends thieves and procurers</u>. His headquarters is the Mexico-City bar, a <u>meeting place for prostitutes and sailors</u>. He conducts his business at the bar, where he waits for the occasional *bourgeois* tourist to enter. *La Chute* is the story of his life, told in the form of a confession to an unnamed and silent tourist.

During his years in Paris, Clamence was content with his life and felt in harmony with the world. His health was excellent, he had many friends, and he was attractive to women. Since he enjoyed being charitable and kind to others, he felt at ease with his conscience. Most important, he was certain of his power:

> No, as a result of being showered with blessings, I felt, I hesitate to admit, marked out. Personally marked out, among all, for that long and uninterrupted success. . . . I literally soared for a period of years, for which, to tell the truth, I still long in my heart of hearts.[1]

One night, as he was returning home across the Pont des Arts, Clamence heard a laugh of derision. He could not tell from where it came, and he felt that the world was laughing at him; his facade of happiness, innocence, and self-contentment crumbled. From this point Clamence dates his fall from the Eden of his youth. Later he confesses that there was an earlier incident on a bridge in Paris, which explains his sudden attack of uncertainty. On the earlier occasion Clamence saw a young girl leaning over a railing. As he proceeded on his way, she jumped into the water and cried for help. He made no effort to rescue her.

Clamence realises that he was cowardly; to avoid facing his conscience he plays various roles. At first, he acts the fool:

> I planned to puncture the tyres of wheelchairs, to go and shout 'lousy proletarian' under the scaffoldings on which labourers were working, to smack infants in the subway.[2]

Later he turns to orgies of drunkenness and sexual debauchery. He remains haunted by his loss of self-respect. He is subject to delusions, mistaking a bit of debris in the ocean for a drowned body. He finally leaves Paris and becomes an exile in Amsterdam, a city which he hates for its dampness, but which he chooses as a means of self-mortification. In Amsterdam he becomes a "judge-penitent." In this role he regains a measure of self-confidence. Once he has confessed his shortcomings to strangers, he then turns the tables and judges the guilt of others.

In *La Chute*, as in Camus's other work, a man becomes aware of life's absurdity. Clamence experiences a disillusionment similar to that of Meursault when he was forced to abandon his studies, or of Tarrou when he realised the terror of capital punishment. Clamence sees the discrepancy between reality and his youthful desires. He believed in his own innocence and strength, and in a world that would allow him to live happily; suddenly he is unsure of himself, and he feels that a hostile universe is laughing at him. He finds that his body may disobey his wishes; on the bridge a "bodily weakness" paralyses him, and he cannot help the drowning girl.

Awakening to absurdity, according to Camus, is the

first step towards a fruitful rebellion. After a man becomes aware of his dissatisfaction with the world, he
rebels in order to establish such values as human dignity,
beauty, happiness. Clamence's rebellion immediately
miscarries, because it has no such positive base; Clamence values nothing and he has lost all self-respect. He is
frightened by the need to make choices in a world that
lacks absolute laws. His career after his fall from innocence is a series of unsuccessful attempts to create a
system of absolute morality.

Clamence cannot admit that self-knowledge is relative.
When he realises that he is not innocent, he decides that
he is absolutely guilty. He re-examines his earlier life;
every act that he thought virtuous now seems to reveal a
profound self-centredness. He felt satisfied in his sexual
relationships; now he sees that they were attempts to
dominate others. His aid to victims of injustice now
appears to have been a means of self-aggrandisement. He
thought that he was innocent and just; he now realises he
was a hypocrite. Because he prefers guilt to uncertainty,
Clamence judges himself and others by impossibly high
standards. He decides that even Christ was guilty, because His life was saved by the massacre of the Innocents.

In *L'Homme révolté* Camus says that the true rebel wants
to love fully and to possess unendingly, but that this is impossible in a world where lovers are often separated and
where all human beings change. Clamence has felt this
longing for absolute love, but, because he has no self-
respect, he interprets such rebellious desires as signs of his
guilt rather than as signs of the hostility of the external
world. Rebellion sounds despicable as Clamence describes it:

On my own admission, I could live happily only on
condition that all the individuals on earth, or the
greatest possible number, were turned towards me,
eternally unattached, deprived of any separate exis-

tence and ready to answer my call at any moment,
doomed in short to sterility until the day I should deign
to favour them. In short, for me to live happily it was
essential for the individuals I chose not to live at all.
They must receive their life, sporadically, only at my
bidding.[3]

Clamence is unable to accept himself; his revolt, rather
than turning outward to change the world, turns inward.
He wants a radical transformation of himself, even if this
leads to his enslavement.

Clamence accepts his own absolute guilt. Because he
cannot believe in God, he must find a new judge. He
realises that this need to be judged is a dominant feature
of his generation. According to Clamence, Christians
have denied the redemptive power of Christ; their
religion has become a means of judgment. Those who do
not accept Christianity have found new systems for
judging men:

Over the dead body of innocence the judges swarm, the
judges of all species, those of Christ and those of the
Anti-Christ who are the same anyway.[4]

Since there is no universally accepted judge, Clamence
himself becomes a "judge-penitent" and proclaims the
guilt of all men. He chooses the name of Jean-Baptiste,
because he wishes to be the prophet of a new religion of
guilt and slavery that will rule the world and save him
from the painful stirrings of his conscience:

But on the bridges of Paris I too learned that I was
afraid of freedom. So hurrah for the master, whoever
he may be, to take the place of heaven's law. . . . In
short, you see, the essential is to cease being free and
to obey, in repentance, a greater rogue than oneself.
When we are all guilty, that will be democracy.[5]

Clamence is initially an attractive figure, whose
analyses of the problems of contemporary life often recall

those in Camus's essays. He goes into a moral decline,
however, after his failure of courage. His last speeches,
justifying a coming kingdom of universal guilt, are
almost maniacal. He becomes odious as he argues for the
enslavement of man. His story is an illustration of the
perversion of rebellion in the contemporary world. Because he has nothing to preserve, no love of the external
world, no personal dignity, Clamence loses the tension of
rebellion. His revolt is an absolute "no," which leads him
to desire destruction and tyranny. His story shows how
the modern world has failed to come to terms with the
loss of established values. Rather than find the courage to
live in a godless world, contemporary rebels, according
to Camus, prefer to erect new, tyrannical divinities.

Clamence's story follows the history of metaphysical
rebellion that Camus traces in *L'Homme révolté*. Metaphysical rebellion begins when men recognise the senseless
evil upon which society and the universe are based.
Early metaphysical rebels, such as the Romantics, recognised their lack of power to change the world; they were
content to appear as evil opponents of a cruel God. Since
later metaphysical rebels denied the existence of God,
they needed to act. The Surrealists, the successors of the
Romantics, sought violently to overthrow the existing
order by a denial of normal sensory experiences. They
wanted an immediate and passionate revolt. When quick
results could not be attained, some rebels turned to the
gradual construction of a new social order; they were
willing to suppress their own needs and passions, and
even to deny human nature, to work for some future
perfection. When he first realises that life is not wholly
good, Clamence, like the Romantic dandy, exults in his
own evil. He wants to appear a ridiculous figure and to
find his identity by making other men judge him:

Since I was a liar, I would reveal this and hurl my
duplicity in the face of all those imbeciles, even before

they discovered it. ... In order to forestall the
laughter, I dreamed of hurling myself into the general
derision.[6]

When this method does not work, Clamence tries to forget his guilt and dissatisfaction by losing his identity in
drunken orgies and sexual debauchery:

At a certain degree of lucid intoxication, lying late at
night between two prostitutes and drained of all
desire, hope ceases to be a torture, you see, the mind
dominates the whole past, and the pain of living is for
ever over.[7]

Clamence's debauchery is a means of attaining an
illusory immortality. This stage of his life suggests a
parallel to the Surrealist movement, which Camus describes as a mysticism without God, a violent and passionate attempt "to melt contradictions in the fire of desire
and love, and to make the walls of death fall."[8] Because
his body cannot stand the strain, Clamence must give up
his life of debauchery. He moves to Amsterdam where he
becomes a prophet of a coming kingdom of guilt and
works to establish a totalitarian system. This system
shares the outstanding feature of present-day Marxism,
as Camus describes it in *L'Homme révolté*:

At the end of this long insurrection, in the name of
human innocence, there arises, by an inevitable perversion of fact, the affirmation of general culpability.
Every man is a criminal who is unaware of being so.[9]

Clamence is not, however, truly a Marxist. Camus
uses him as a symbol of the French intellectual's flirta-
tion with Marxism. Camus wrote *La Chute* at a time
when he was disillusioned with left-wing political thought
in post-war France. Clamence's career is a satire on the
self-induced impotence of contemporary radicalism. Because the novel was often misinterpreted, Camus, to
underline the satiric intent, added an epigraph to the

English translation of *La Chute*, from Lermontov's *A Hero of our Time*:

> *A Hero of our Time*, gentlemen, is in fact a portrait but not of an individual; it is the aggregate of the vices of our whole generation in their fullest expression.

Camus includes himself in the generation to be satirised, and in many ways Clamence resembles him. A friend of Camus's has remarked: "Never had any of his other heroes spoken to us in a voice where we could recognise so well the voice of a certain Camus—ironic, mocking, and familiar."[10] Clamence shares Camus's disapproval of Christianity and of modern Parisian society, as well as his love of sports and of the theatre. His career in Paris before his fall sometimes suggests parallels to Camus's earlier writings. Clamence defends "noble murderers,"[11] as Camus defends Caligula, Martha, and Meursault. The list of subjects that Clamence accuses himself of treating superficially is a summary of Camus's principal themes:

> Fundamentally, nothing mattered. War, suicide, love, poverty got my attention, of course, when circumstances forced me, but a courteous, superficial attention.[12]

When Clamence criticises the moral attitude behind his easy success in Paris, one feels that perhaps Camus is attacking himself. Camus's work of the immediate post-war period was concerned with advocating a new approach to political morality and he quickly reached literary fame. Like Clamence, who is a respected lawyer arguing for humanitarian causes, Camus was regarded as a moral guide for the younger generation. With the publication of *L'Homme révolté* the situation changed sharply. Camus was frequently under attack, and he replied with vehemence to his critics. Sartre and his colleague, Francis Jeanson, denounced Camus for his self-righteous attitude,

and there is some justice in their remarks. In his reply to
Sartre, Camus said that criticism of *L'Homme révolté* is an
attack on the hopes of his generation. In the autobio-
graphical preface to *L'Envers et l'endroit* (1958), he admits
that he may have sometimes appeared to be self-
righteous:

> If I have, at this moment, the impression of having
> made a mistake or of having lied in what I sometimes
> wrote, it is because I don't know how honestly to make
> known my injustice. No doubt I never said I was just.
> Only sometimes I would say that we must try to be
> just, and also that this was a difficult task. But is the
> difference so great? And can anyone preach justice who
> can't even manage to make it reign in his own life?[13]

In *La Chute* Camus appears to recognise that in his own
life outward virtue may have hidden moral failings.

If there is a recognition in *La Chute* that moral guilt
exists, there is also a recognition that man's feelings of
guilt can be manipulated to justify despotism. If there is
self-criticism in *La Chute*, there is a much stronger and
more severe attack on those who criticised Camus. *La
Chute* is, in fact, partly an answer to Sartre's criticism of
L'Homme révolté. Clamence is best understood as a figure
who, unlike Camus, accepts the criticisms of Sartre and
Jeanson, and whose feelings of guilt lead to moral de-
generation. When Clamence comments upon his past, he
often echoes, in an ironic fashion, some of the criticisms
made in *Les Temps modernes* about Camus's character and
moral attitudes. Clamence refers to his half-read books
(an allusion to Sartre's claim that Camus read neither
Sartre nor Hegel before writing *L'Homme révolté*). Clamence, who likes the imperfect subjunctive (a tense seldom
used in modern French), reproaches himself for his fine
speech:

> I am well aware that an addiction to silk underwear

does not necessarily imply that one's feet are dirty. Nonetheless, style, like sheer silk, too often hides eczema. My consolation is to tell myself that, after all, those who murder the language are not pure either.[14]

Jeanson attacked *L'Homme révolté* for the classicism of its style, which, he said, could not disguise the muddled thought.[15]

Jeanson also criticised Camus for being so concerned with metaphysical rebellion that he was politically ineffective; Camus had not moved to the political right: "You aren't on the right, Camus, you're in the air."[16] When he mentions his passion for heights, Clamence humorously echoes this criticism. He prefers the bus to the underground, he paces the top deck while on ship. He likes being on terraces above the mass of "human ants." Clamence's professional activity is based on a love of high altitudes:

Just consider this, *cher* Monsieur, I lived with impunity. I was concerned in no judgment; I was not on the floor of the courtroom but somewhere in the flies like those gods that are brought down by machinery from time to time to transfigure the action and give it its meaning. After all, living aloft is still the only way of being seen and hailed by the largest number.[17]

From his acceptance of such criticism, Clamence develops a strong feeling of guilt. In showing how guilt leads to tyranny, Camus satirises what he felt was the tendency of Sartre's political philosophy. In his reply to *Les Temps modernes*, Camus criticises the position of left-wing intellectuals who attempt to justify the politics of the Soviet Union. He claims that many intellectuals are so ashamed of being *bourgeois* that they are willing to give up their liberty to criticise:

There is, in fact, repentance in the case of these bour-

G

geois intellectuals who want to expiate their origins, even at the price of contradiction and violence to their intelligence.[18]

According to Camus, Sartre's revolt is perverted by a feeling of guilt, which makes him afraid of liberty. Since he cannot accept a transcendental morality, Sartre chooses a Marxist interpretation of history. This gives him a new absolute system and obviates any need for personal freedom of choice. Sartre moves "according to the law of nihilism, from extreme liberty to extreme necessity; this is nothing else but dedicating oneself to making slaves."[19]

Clamence's role as "judge-penitent" is thus meant as a satire on Existentialist methods.[20] Sartre's work attacks his *bourgeois* readers. In *Qu'est-ce que la littérature?* Sartre states his purpose in terms quite close to those of Clamence: "The function of the writer is to work so that no one can call himself innocent."[21] Clamence confesses his own guilt so that he may judge others; his preferred audience is "the bourgeois, and the straying bourgeois at that."[22] Like Sartre, who often writes in left-bank cafés, Clamence lies in wait for his audience at the Mexico-City bar.

In *L'Homme révolté* Camus says that modern revolutionaries, who sacrifice the present for some future perfection, create a Hell on earth. Clamence, who shares this revolutionary desire to transform reality, creates his own Hell. His story, in fact, contains many echoes of Dante's *Inferno*. Clamence sees himself as a guide who, like Virgil, takes his listener on a tour of the Ninth Circle of Hell. Amsterdam is, Clamence explains, the last circle of a modern Hell:

The middle-class hell, of course, peopled with bad dreams. When one comes from the outside, as one gradually goes through those circles, life—and hence its crimes—becomes denser, darker. Here, we are in the last circle. The circle of the . . . Ah, you know that?[23]

With characteristic irony, Camus omits the key word "traitors"; only gradually are we aware that Clamence has committed a form of treason.

As Dante begins his descent into the Ninth Circle, he sees the giant Nimrod, the reputed builder of the Tower of Babel. Nimrod speaks no intelligible language. Clamence begins his story at the Mexico-City bar, which is managed by a "worthy gorilla" who speaks only Dutch, and who cannot understand the sailors of various nationalities who frequent the bar. "Fancy the Cro-Magnon man lodged in the Tower of Babel!"[24] (Interestingly enough, a Mexico-City bar in fact does exist at Warmoesstraat 91, in the section of Amsterdam known as the Dam. When I visited the bar in 1958, I was told that Camus had written part of his manuscript there and had sent the management a copy of *La Chute*. At the time of Camus's visit, the bar was managed by a muscular ex-sailor who spoke only Dutch.)

Just as Dante descends through three rings of the Ninth Circle before reaching the inner ring of Judecca, reserved for the greatest traitors, so Clamence takes his listener through three sections of Amsterdam, and then to his own room. Dante's Hell is a place of supernatural cold and supernatural heat; in his room Clamence feels both extremes of temperature: "Open the window a little, please; it's frightfully hot. Not too much, I'm cold as well."[25] Clamence wants to escape into the open air, but he cannot move. He is no longer a guide; he has become a modern Satan, imprisoned in his own Hell:

I sit enthroned among my bad angels at the summit of the Dutch heaven and I watch ascending towards me, as they issue from the fogs and the water, the multitude of the Last Judgment. They rise slowly; I already see the first of them arriving. On his bewildered face, half hidden by a hand, I read the melancholy of the common condition and the despair of not being able to escape it. And as for me, I pity without absolving, I understand without forgiving and, above all, I feel at last that I am being adored![26]

Clamence, like Satan, becomes a traitor after he falls from innocence. He commits treason against his fellow men by proclaiming universal guilt.

Clamence does not see himself as Satan, but as John the Baptist announcing redemption based on an awareness of sin. He dresses like John the Baptist: "The camel that provided the hair for my overcoat may have been mangy."[27] He calls himself a prophet crying in the wilderness. Like John the Baptist, he compares himself with Elijah, and he tries to make the doves descend from heaven as they did at Christ's baptism. Clamence is, however, incapable of asceticism or self-sacrifice and he is morbidly afraid of water, which represents for him the death of his ego rather than baptismal salvation. He is only a false prophet. He is not Elijah, nor can he make the doves descend from heaven:

See the huge flakes drifting against the window-panes. It must be the doves, surely. They finally make up their minds to come down, the little dears. . . . Come now, admit that you would be flabbergasted if a chariot came down from heaven to carry me off, or if the snow suddenly caught fire. You don't believe it? No more do I.[28]

Clamence is basically a comedian playing with words and gestures on the surface of life. He surrounds himself with stage effects in a desperate attempt to regain his self-respect, but he is not successful in any of his roles. He plays his Satanic role in a shabby bar in a poor section of Amsterdam. Although he neglects the drowning woman, he does nothing else of an overtly shocking nature. He is less guilty than Meursault. Rather than openly create a

story of despair, rather than directly express his personal
bitterness or the larger tragedy of modern politics, Camus
chooses to write in a deliberately ironic and understated
fashion. *La Chute* mocks the moral tragedy of contemporary life.

Clamence's story is an image of the dangers inherent
in the metaphysical aspirations of contemporary political
philosophy. The structural elements of the novel con-
verge to give a stylised form to the theme of the work.
The physical background of mist and fog, the setting in
the concentric and spiralling circles of Hell, the many
allusions to water and drowning, the precipitous nature
of the talk, create an image of a whirlpool that symbolises
the moral void of modern man caught in the snares of his
own thought. *La Chute* is a picture of a contemporary Hell
created from the perversion of rebellion.

Although *La Chute* does not represent a radical change
in Camus's philosophy, it does create a darker and more
pessimistic atmosphere than his earlier works. *La Peste*,
Les Justes, and *L'Homme révolté* offer at least a provisional
ethic; *La Chute* shows only false solutions. Neither Christianity nor Marxist Existentialism can save man. If any
salvation is possible, it is only through the ability to
escape from one's ego, an ability which Clamence does
not have:

> One would have to cease being anyone, forget oneself
> for someone else, at least once. But how? Don't be too
> hard on me. . . . Yes, we have lost track of the light,
> the mornings, the holy innocence of those who forgive
> themselves.[29]

La Chute does not suggest that such innocence can be re-
captured. The bitterness lying beneath the comedy and
the refusal to formulate a more positive attitude are perhaps the clearest indications of the extent to which
Camus changed as a result of his experiences after the
War.

REFERENCES

1. *C.*, pp. 36–7 (23).
2. *C.*, p. 107 (68).
3. *C.*, pp. 79–80 (50–1).
4. *C.*, p. 134 (86).
5. *C.*, p. 157 (100–1).
6. *C.*, p. 106 (68).
7. *C.*, pp. 118–19 (76).
8. *H.R.*, p. 126 (not translated in English edition).
9. *H.R.*, p. 229 (212).
10. Jean-Claude Brisville, *Camus*, p. 72.
11. *C.*, p. 26 (16).
12. *C.*, p. 59 (38).
13. *E.E.*, pp. 28–9.
14. *C.*, p. 10 (7).
15. Francis Jeanson, "Albert Camus ou l'âme révoltée" (1952), p. 2072.
16. Francis Jeanson, "Pour tout vous dire . . ." (1952), p. 372.
17. *C.*, pp. 32–3 (21).
18. *Actuelles II*, p. 113.
19. *Op. cit.*, p. 117.
20. See Dominique Aury, "A Talk with Albert Camus" (1957), p. 33.
21. Sartre, *Qu'est-ce que la littérature?* (1948), p. 74.
22. *C.*, p. 160 (102).
23. *C.*, pp. 19–20 (13).
24. *C.*, p. 8 (5).
25. *C.*, p. 159 (101).
26. *C.*, p. 165 (105–6).
27. *C.*, p. 14 (9).
28. *C.*, pp. 167–8 (107).
29. *C.*, p. 167 (107).

CHAPTER VII

PLAYS AND STORIES

Camus's plays are less successful than his novels. In spite of his passionate interest in the theatre, Camus did not have the bold imagination necessary to write first-rate drama. The plots of his plays lack dramatic tension, and the characters are less subtly delineated than those in his novels. Clamence, in *La Chute*, is the most dramatically effective character that Camus created, but Clamence can only function in an armchair monologue. The plays are of interest largely for the insight they offer into Camus's philosophical development.

Caligula, Camus's first play, was written in 1938, but not published or performed until 1945. Caligula is a flamboyant young emperor who reacts violently to a first awareness of "absurdity." He discovers that "men die and they are not happy." This simple truth is not obvious to the Roman patricians, who, like the *bourgeoisie* of Algiers in *L'Etranger*, have interposed a set of masks between themselves and reality. Caligula decides to embark on an educational mission; he will force the patricians to recognise absurdity by acting in a manner as absurd as that of the universe. The play is a series of tableaux illustrating how Caligula destroys the moral values of the patricians, their personal integrity, and their belief in reason. Caligula forces the families of his victims to laugh, he drags a wife from her husband and rapes her, he capriciously kills men, he arbitrarily closes the country's granaries and declares a famine.

He hopes that by acting freely and amorally he can overcome the power of the hostile universe. Just before he

is killed by a patrician uprising, he realises that he has
failed to reach his goal: "I have chosen a wrong path, a
path that leads to nothing. My freedom isn't the right
one."[1] *Caligula* poses a question to which Camus returns
frequently in his later work: In a world with no transcendent meaning, what arguments can be advanced
for respecting human life? The play, however, offers no
clear explanation of why Caligula's path is wrong.

Le Malentendu (1945), Camus's second play, is the story
of Jan, a man who returns home after twenty years of a
rich and happy life abroad. His mother and sister keep an
inn in a depressing central European village. In order to
escape to a warmer country, they murder and rob rich
travellers. Unable to find the right words to identify himself, Jan decides to spend one night in the inn posing as a
stranger. His mother and sister murder him. When she
discovers whom she has killed, his mother commits
suicide. His sister, Martha, who feels that she has been
rejected in favour of the returned prodigal son, also kills
herself. Jan's wife is left alone, with her faith in the meaning and beauty of the universe destroyed.

In *Caligula* Camus does not show that any moral attitude can be drawn from Caligula's discovery of a discrepancy between his desires and external reality.
Similarly, *Le Malentendu* presents a striking image of a
universe without love or hope, but it does not suggest any
way of rebelling fruitfully against such a universe. Both
plays are more bitter and nihilistic than Camus's other
early work.

Camus's later plays, *L'Etat de siège* and *Les Justes* present a more constructive ethic of revolt. *L'Etat de siège*
(1948) is a story of an epidemic and of a community's
reaction to it. The plot bears no similarity, however, to
that of *La Peste*. In *L'Etat de siège* the plague is personified
and appears as a political dictator: as a result the play
seems to be a simple allegory of the German Occupation.
It lacks the complexity and ambiguity of the novel,

and is undoubtedly the least effective of all Camus's works.

Les Justes (1950), Camus's last play, is his best. It is the story of the "fastidious assassins," the Russian revolutionaries of 1905, whom Camus praises in *L'Homme révolté* for the purity of their revolt. The hero of *Les Justes*, Ivan Kaliayev, is a romantic and idealistic revolutionary. His hatred of oppression has not destroyed his belief that men must conduct themselves with honour even when opposing tyranny. Ordered to bomb the Grand-Duke's carriage, Kaliayev refuses because of the unexpected presence of two children in the carriage. When he succeeds in a later assassination attempt, Kaliayev wants to be executed. He rejects an offer of pardon because he feels that his death will restore a moral balance; it will make the assassination an act of justice and not a crime: "If I did not die, then I would be a murderer."[2]

We admire Kaliayev and Dora Doulebov, the woman he loves, for their idealistic strength and for their willingness to die for the revolution. We realise, however, that they want to die, in order to resolve the tension between their desire for love and their desire for justice. In the final scene of the play, after she has heard a detailed account of Kaliayev's bravery on the scaffold, Dora comments: "It is easy, it is so much easier to die from one's inner conflicts than to live with them."[3] *Les Justes* presents the most heroic characters in all of Camus's work, but it shows their limitations. In *Les Justes*, Camus avoids the moralistic attitude that detracts from *L'Etat de siège*.

L'Exil et le royaume (1957), Camus's last creative work, is a group of six short stories. They describe the dual nature of the world, which Camus had first expressed in *L'Envers et l'endroit*: the world is the place of man's exile, but it is also his only kingdom. With one exception, "Le Renégat," the stories are concerned with less violent metaphysical experiences than is Camus's earlier work. In *L'Exil et le royaume* the characters do not feel a profound psychological shock when they first encounter absurdity; through simple experiences they slowly become aware of their dissatisfaction.

"Le Renégat," the least typical of the stories, is closer in theme and treatment to *La Chute* (which Camus originally planned as a short story in *L'Exil et le royaume*). The renegade is a young Catholic priest who is determined to convert a fierce, isolated tribe in the Algerian desert. After much physical torture and spiritual humiliation, he is instead converted to the barbarous religion of the natives. The renegade turns from a religion of love to a religion of hatred and slavery, as Clamence moves from liberal secular opinions to a justification of tyranny. This radical change in the renegade's outlook is motivated by certain pathological traits in his character. He distrusts women and he lacks self-respect; he takes pleasure in feelings of guilt and even in the torture imposed upon him. Since all white men are guilty in the eyes of the natives, he hopes that the native tribe will conquer the whites. He will then be able to join a community of the guilty.

The story is a study of a masochistic character; it is also a parable of the modern acceptance of totalitarianism. The renegade priest shares what Camus terms in *L'Homme révolté* the "Nordic" world view, which Marxism inherited from the Christian tradition. According to such a view, the natural world and human nature are evils to be dominated. Since the renegade sees no beauty in the world and has no respect for himself or for others, he wants to transform reality. When he discovers that the Christian God is not omnipotent, he turns to a stronger power. He hopes to establish an earthly kingdom in which men will be forced into a common mould of guilt. At the end of his confused monologue, the renegade priest is crucified by the natives. He becomes a perverted Christ figure, perhaps the saviour whose coming is prophesied by Jean-Baptiste Clamence.

Janine, the heroine of "La Femme adultère," is a woman of forty, caught in a *petit-bourgeois* routine; she has sacrificed happiness to material security. When she goes with her husband on a sales tour in the Algerian desert, she gradually becomes aware of the vast contrast between her life and that of the nomadic tribes she sees. Janine and her husband are encumbered with material possessions and they have lost most of their physical vitality. Her husband must degrade himself in order to sell his goods. The Arabs live in a physical harmony with the world around them; they have a natural pride in their existence. Late at night Janine escapes from her hotel room. On a terrace overlooking the desert she feels in contact with a purer world. This is her symbolic act of adultery, which is a betrayal of her husband's way of life. She experiences an identity with nature similar to that which Camus describes in *Noces*: a moment when man can feel part of a larger and enduring beauty, when the concerns of material existence seem trivial, and when even death is no longer an enemy. Janine's deliverance is similar to Meursault's acceptance of the "benign indifference of the universe." This deliverance is only temporary, however, for Janine must return to the world of her husband.

"Les Muets" and "L'Hôte" are stories about misunderstanding and social barriers between groups of men. "Les Muets" tells of a quarrel between workers and employer in a small Algerian workshop. Because the shop is no longer economically profitable, the employer cannot meet demands for higher wages. The men are so filled with despair and bitterness that they are unable to sympathise with the employer whose child becomes critically ill. Both employer and employees are imprisoned in a world of exile and death.

Daru, the hero of "L'Hôte," is a schoolmaster in a small village on the Algerian plateau. He is asked to take an Arab prisoner into custody and to deliver him to the police. Although he has little sympathy for the prisoner, who killed another Arab in a brawl, Daru cannot agree to act as a policeman. After one night he sets the prisoner free, showing him the roads to the town where he will be judged and to the hills where nomadic tribes will give him protection. The Arab chooses to surrender. Returning to his school, Daru finds a message: "You handed over our brother. You will pay for this." Neither the Europeans nor the Arabs understand him. "In this vast landscape he had loved so much, he was alone."[4]

"L'Hôte" expresses, indirectly, the tragedy of the Algerian political situation; violence was prevalent on both sides, and both sides demanded complete allegiance from their followers. Daru, who cannot give such allegiance, is faced with a dilemma similar to Camus's. Like Camus, Daru finds only a painfully solitary course of action that seems to be a way of avoiding responsibility. The political problem is deliberately simplified in "L'Hôte." Daru is required only to hand over one prisoner whose crime was not political. The indirect handling of moral issues is similar to that in *La Peste*, where violent warfare against other men is symbolised by a fight against the natural universe.

"Jonas, ou l'artiste au travail" begins as a humorous satire on literary and artistic society in Paris. Gilbert Jonas, a painter, is exploited by his dealer; his acquaintances cultivate him for social prestige. Jonas has little time in which to paint; he also has little space. His small apartment is filled with babies, canvases, and visitors. A turning point occurs when he realises the dangers of being a famous artist and tries to escape. He begins several casual love affairs, he spends most of his time in bars, he neglects his art. When his experiment of living in unrestricted freedom is not successful, Jonas returns home to work. In the crowded apartment he builds a loft, where he can be alone and yet hear his family below him. Since he refuses to eat, he falls unconscious from the loft.

He leaves one canvas with a word painted on it. No one can tell "whether it should be read *solitary* or *solidary*."[5]

As his name suggests, Gilbert Jonas, the painter, bears many similarities to Albert Camus, the novelist. Jonas is married two years before attaining sudden fame; Camus was married in 1940, two years before the publication of *L'Etranger*. Jonas's wife "produced, in rapid succession, two children, a boy and a girl."[6] Francine Camus gave birth to twins, a boy and a girl, in 1945. Like Camus, Jonas lives for his art and believes strongly in a personal "star" that will guide him. He faces the problems that, according to Camus, confront all artists in contemporary society. He tries to balance his family life and his need for creative solitude. As Camus says in his Nobel Prize speech:

> The artist fashions himself in that ceaseless oscillation from himself to others, midway between the beauty he cannot do without and the community from which he cannot tear himself.[7]

The artist should not work in isolation from the problems of his time, nor should he be so much a part of his society that he cannot see beyond it. Jonas's loft is a humorous symbol of the artist's balance.

"La Pierre qui pousse," the final story of *L'Exil et le royaume*, tells of D'Arrast, a French engineer who goes to Brazil to construct a dam. D'Arrast has rejected his *bourgeois* culture, where "the masters are policemen or merchants,"[8] but he does not feel at home among the people of Brazil. He sees that the white ruling class is riddled with petty prejudices, but he cannot fully understand the elemental frenzy of the uneducated Negroes. During a religious festival, one of the Negroes attempts to fulfil a vow by carrying a heavy rock in a procession to the church. When he stumbles and falls, D'Arrast picks up his rock, but instead of completing the journey to the church, he carries the rock to a native cabin and deposits

it on the hearth. Although no one understands the reason
for his act, the Negroes invite him to eat with them.
D'Arrast temporarily overcomes his feeling of exile and
solitude.

"La Pierre qui pousse" is the longest and most am-
bitious story in *L'Exil et le royaume*. Camus attempts to
create a myth of the condition of modern man. Carrying
the rock represents the patient effort of men to overcome
the racial, cultural and economic barriers between them.
Like the task of Sisyphus, however, D'Arrast's act is
gratuitous, because it is directed against the gods and
offers no hope of eternal salvation. The kingdom is
always a temporary construction within the exile.

Camus considered these stories as experiments towards
a more realistic narrative form. In his novels, he often
portrays life's absurdity through bizarre characters or
unusual incidents. In *L'Exil et le royaume*, he chooses to
show the tensions of modern life through more commonplace experiences. It is difficult to say whether such an
approach would have proved fruitful for Camus in later
work. The stories in *L'Exil et le royaume* are sometimes
awkward in language and structure; with the exception
of "L'Hôte," they are below the level of his novels and
essays.

REFERENCES

1. *Caligula*, p. 226 (*Caligula* and
   Cross Purpose, tr. S. Gilbert,
   p. 94).
2. *Les Justes*, p. 145.
3. *Op. cit.*, p. 169.
4. *L'Exil et le royaume*, p. 124
   (*Exile and the Kingdom*, tr. J.
   O'Brien, p. 84).
5. *Op. cit.*, p. 176 (118).
6. *Op. cit.*, p. 136 (90).
7. *Discours de Suède*, p. 13
   (translated in *Resistance, Rebellion and Death*, tr. J.
   O'Brien, p. 196).
8. *L'Exil et le royaume*, p. 202
   (135).

CHAPTER VIII

CAMUS AND HIS CRITICS

In France many critics of Camus, whether hostile or friendly, have discussed his personality rather than the quality of his writing. Such an attack as Anne Durand's *Le Cas Albert Camus* is extremely bitter; Miss Durand makes many unpleasant assumptions about Camus's life. One group of Surrealist intellectuals even devoted the first issue of its magazine, *Le Soleil noir*, to a virulent refutation of the concept of limited revolt that Camus developed in *L'Homme révolté*. Praise is often equally extreme. Camus had a strong moral influence on many younger writers, and several of them wrote eulogistic essays on his work and character. Jacques Chauviré, who corresponded with Camus, wrote a novel, *Les Passants*, in which the hero is given moral guidance by letters from Camus. After Camus's death, a group of type-setters and proof-readers who had worked with him on various newspapers wrote a book of reminiscences about him.

Camus has perhaps attracted more attention among Catholic critics than any other non-Christian writer of the post-war period. Upon first reading *L'Etranger* some Catholic critics thought that Meursault was pathological, a monster who lacked moral sensitivity and intelligence. Camus was accused of deliberately describing experience at a less than human level to prove his theory of life's absurdity. Although *La Peste* is Camus's most openly anti-Christian book, it was more acceptable to many Catholic critics, who saw in it a return to traditional humanistic values with which the Church could sympathise.

Because Clamence recognises original sin and awaits a

saviour, many Catholic critics see in *La Chute* signs that Camus was approaching conversion at the time of his death. To read the novel in this way, one must discount its satiric implications, and some critics have obviously been willing to do so. Even Pierre-Henri Simon, one of the more perceptive and sympathetic of Camus's left-wing Catholic critics, while realising that *La Chute* is ironic, feels that the preoccupation with sin and redemption is not merely on the surface, and that it might have led to conversion had Camus lived.

The concept of revolt developed in *L'Etranger* and *Le Mythe de Sisyphe* brought Camus the admiration of many secular left-wing intellectuals who later felt that the philosophy of *La Peste* and *L'Homme révolté* was too conservative. While Sartre wrote one of the best early essays on *L'Etranger*, critics in his magazine *Les Temps modernes* attacked the moral attitude behind *La Peste*; they felt that Camus did not face the problems of rebellion against the present social order, and they claimed that his use of the plague as an allegory for the Occupation misrepresented the nature of the Resistance movement. According to such critics, Camus describes rebellion against injustice as if it were a simple community activity similar to aiding victims of natural disasters; they claim he does not recognise that rebellion necessitates a political commitment to fight against other men.

Left-wing critics have frequently felt that, as his revolt against the universe became less violent, Camus's thought grew fuzzy and his creative powers declined. According to Robert Kanters, Camus's most fruitful period was that of *L'Etranger* and *Le Mythe de Sisyphe*, when he expressed the despair of a whole generation and found in that despair reasons for a continued vitality. Camus later became such a "friend of mankind" that he could only express the soft truths of a vaguely left-wing humanism:

The excellence of his first books perhaps arises from

their internal tension, from the contradiction between the absolute despair of Camus's thought and his desperate love of life. But we must admit that the dialectic of rebellion through which he tries to escape from this contradiction satisfies neither the demands of reason nor the demands of a heart enamoured of absolute revolt. His dialectic is a reassuring conversion; he settles down, forsaking desperate thought for the ideas of a good family man. With great and noble words he channels the energy of death to make it irrigate our dear moderate slopes.[1]

According to Kanters, Camus is the last saint of *petit-bourgeois* grandeur.

Many critics are guilty of ignoring the impact of Camus's fiction and of reducing its tensions to simplified theses that easily can be praised or refuted. In doing so, they sometimes falsify his thought. Catholic critics often do not recognise the complicated satiric perspective of *La Chute*; left-wing intellectuals usually discount the ambiguity of *La Peste*. It is equally wrong to read *L'Homme révolté* and all of Camus's later work as an expression of moderate liberalism. Much of his later fiction, including *La Chute*, "Le Renégat" and "L'Hôte," expresses a profound despair. Even the moderate revolt that he advocates in *L'Homme révolté* is a difficult balance between despair and hope. If it does not constitute a call to immediate revolutionary action, it is not a retreat into simple "good feelings." Camus develops a useful moral corrective to cynicism; he shows his contemporaries that from intense despair one can deduce reasons for living with dignity, and this is one basis for his strong moral influence upon his generation. While he exposes the perversions to which some left-wing thought has been subject, he does not turn to conservatism. Camus's views on the problem of Algerian independence can legitimately be attacked as unrealistic and as prejudiced in favour of the

European population. But his basic moral position is admirable; he avoids becoming an apologist for violence, and he refuses to accept the sacrifice of the present for the future.

Examined from the point of view of formal philosophy, Camus's essays have obvious weaknesses. Sartre remarks that Camus inaccurately reads the philosophies of Husserl (in *Le Mythe de Sisyphe*) and Hegel (in *L'Homme révolté*). A. J. Ayer claims that Camus's demand for order and clarity can never be fulfilled, that the argument of *Le Mythe de Sisyphe* is romantic rather than logical. John Cruickshank and Philip Thody claim that there are logical flaws in the arguments of *Le Mythe de Sisyphe* and *L'Homme révolté*, and Thody suggests that much of Camus's thought in *L'Homme révolté* is not original.

Although these criticisms contain some truth, they do not deal with the particular qualities of Camus's essays. Unlike Sartre, Camus is not a professional philosopher. *Le Mythe de Sisyphe* and *L'Homme révolté* cannot be read as formal philosophy; Camus's arguments are not as rigorously logical as he tries to make them appear, nor does he develop a new ontological system. In neither *Le Mythe de Sisyphe* nor *L'Homme révolté* does he make a comprehensive historical survey of modern philosophy; his concern is limited to those writers who have influenced European radical intellectuals. If Camus occasionally oversimplifies some theories, he is not primarily interested in formal expositions of philosophical thought. If some of the ideas in *L'Homme révolté* are derived from other analysts of political thought, Camus uses them as the basis for developing his personal moral position. He sees a dangerous lack of moderation in contemporary left-wing thought, but he does not use this tendency to justify a retreat to conservatism. Instead he establishes a personal idea of measure, based upon the dual reaction to the world that he described in *Noces*: rebellion against injustice is balanced by a consent to the beauty of the existing world.

Camus's moderation is not a placid willingness to play it safe, but a tense emotional commitment both to be constantly aware of what is worth saving and to be aware of what must be destroyed.

In his philosophical and lyric essays, Camus's passionate concern with moral problems is more forceful than the logic of his arguments. He was faced with a world that seemed to him unbearably cruel because its beauty is temporary and because its promise of happiness is cut short by death. He found that his fellow men were blind to this basic reality, that they sacrificed immediate pleasures to further abstract historical and religious systems, and that they misused their reason to find justifications of violence. His essays convey his sense of outrage at this affront to human dignity. Even if despair is a constant condition of humanity, Camus wants man to fight for happiness. *Le Mythe de Sisyphe*, *L'Homme révolté* and *Noces* record a persistent duality in the human psyche: man's desire to rebel against injustice and his need for peace. Camus refuses to suppress either of these states. Because of his warm but lucid presentation of his thought, his essays have a value surpassing any importance as documents of their age. If they do not belong to the realm of academic philosophy, they are nevertheless important instances of moral philosophy.

Many English and American books on Camus are either general summaries of his philosophy or elementary explications of his novels as illustrations of his thought. The first book on Camus in English, Philip Thody's *Albert Camus* (1957), was largely an apologetic and over-simplified explanation for English readers. Thody's second book, *Albert Camus: 1913–1960* (1961), is a much better analysis of the chronological development of Camus's thought and art; it contains the most complete biographical information on Camus yet available. Thody perhaps errs in his underestimation of the originality and value of *L'Homme révolté*. While he gives sensible and accurate interpretations of the themes of Camus's novels, he does not appreciate their total artistic impact. Indeed, few critics have examined Camus's strength as a novelist. John Cruickshank's *Albert Camus and the Literature of Revolt* contains a good analysis of Camus's thought and of some literary techniques in *L'Etranger* and *La Peste*, but in general his treatment of Camus's fiction, especially *La Chute* and *L'Exil et le royaume*, is sketchy. These books are, however, at least equal to the best general work in French on Camus: Roger Quilliot's *La Mer et les prisons*.

Many studies of Camus's fiction have their origins in Sartre's brilliant early essay. Sartre examines the formal structure of *L'Etranger* and the techniques through which Camus conveys a sense of absurdity. Sartre claims that by using an outsider as a narrator (Meursault is neither *bourgeois* nor Arab), Camus shows the hypocrisy of social conventions. Sartre points to the lack of causal conjunctions in Meursault's narrative. Meursault never uses "because" or "since"; he merely juxtaposes statements, because he sees no rational causation in the world. Sartre also analyses the effect of Camus's use of the *passé composé*, a tense not normally used in literary French. This compound tense conveys, Sartre feels, a sense of isolated moments and disconnected events. He shows that Camus's literary devices are closely related to Meursault's philosophical outlook. Robert Champigny's *Sur un héros païen*, a stimulating interpretation of *L'Etranger*, also follows a philosophical approach, studying Meursault as an exemplar of epicurean thought. English and American studies of imagery and techniques in Camus's novels have often branched off from Sartre's philosophical approach to consider the mythic and Freudian elements in Camus's fiction. As Carl Viggiani has remarked, Camus followed in the tradition of Eliot and Joyce, using myth self-consciously and ironically.[2] Anglo-Saxon critics have often been more alert than French critics to this feature of Camus's writing. Such detailed studies demonstrate that

Camus's fiction is more than a simple illustration of a philosophical thesis and by showing the richness of imagery and allusion in his writing, they help to evaluate Camus's achievement.

Gaëtan Picon, one of Camus's more perceptive critics, feels that because it is too abstract and schematised Camus's fiction never fulfils its promise: imagery in *La Chute* is used only to underline meaning, dialogues in *La Peste* are stylised intellectual arguments. According to Picon, Camus's passion for artistic unity betrays the richness of his experience:

> *The Stranger, The Plague, The Fall* all contain effective myths, rigorous thoughts, but because of that unity which is reflected by the single word in their titles, they destroy the rhythmical truth of a life seeking to know itself.[3]

In claiming that Camus's experience is richer than is suggested by his novels, Picon is in agreement with the preface to *L'Envers et l'endroit* in which Camus says that the high barriers he erects between his experience and its expression in his work create a certain rigidity that he would like to eliminate.

Because of the Continental tradition of philosophical tales, French critics have the advantage of being able to place Camus's fiction within established *genres*. Sartre mentions the affinities of *L'Etranger* to Voltaire's *contes*; Pierre-Henri Simon makes a similar comment:

> by his scorn of anecdote and of unnecessary detail, by his tendency to humour, and by his interest in playing with symbolic marionettes rather than in manipulating human depth, Camus appeared less as a novelist than as a *conteur*.[4]

Because they lack such a tradition of *contes*, English and American critics often reject the philosophical nature of Camus's fiction. Angus Wilson believes that Camus

tends to "crush the life out of his creations" and that this
results from a reprehensibly abstract interest in humanity:

> the love of mankind or humanity has never been a
> satisfactory humanism; only an intensity of feeling—
> love mixed with hatred—for individual men and
> women, an innate sociability, can prevent the human-
> ist from taking flight into the abstract, from drawing
> men and women according to his own hopes and
> fears.[5]

Irving Howe makes a similar criticism when he says that
Camus wants to write an allegory in an age without an
accepted ideology upon which it can be based; conse-
quently Camus lacks clear images or precise ideas
through which to express his thought:

> To some extent, I would imagine, this reflects the
> dilemma of those post-Resistance intellectuals in
> France who refused to surrender themselves to any
> total ideology yet felt a need for some principle by
> which to guide their public life. Their earlier hopes
> dissipated, they soon began to fall back upon senti-
> ments of fraternity, sentiments without which little
> else can be worthwhile but which in themselves cannot
> lead to concrete realizations in either life or art.
> Perhaps that is why Camus's reflections tend to go
> soft and vague, and why his fiction seems thin-blooded,
> abstract and willed.[6]

While it is true that there are no detailed social settings in Camus's novels, it is also true that he did not
intend to reproduce the rich flux of daily life. The extreme order that he imposed upon his fiction, the
absence of unnecessary detail, the repetition of a few
basic themes, were meant to show his contempt for the
lack of order in the universe. Artistic control was for him
an expression of revolt against the formlessness of reality.
Camus intended to write tales that would symbolise his

view of man's metaphysical condition. He chose powerful symbols for the hostile forces of the universe and created heroes who convincingly embody a contemporary spirit of rebellion against the universe. If his stories are myths of the human condition, they are never dry allegories.

Camus wrote perhaps the best French prose since Gide. His mastery of style can be seen both in his essays and in his fiction. The clarity and measured cadences of his language in *L'Homme révolté* attain poetic character. His descriptions of the Algerian landscape in *Noces* have their own lyric beauty. Through images of the natural world Camus recreates the harshness of reality:

> I seemed to clap in the wind like a mast. With hollowed cheeks, my eyes burning and my lips cracking, my skin dried up until it no longer seemed to be mine. Up to this moment I had been able to decipher with it the language of the elements. They had traced on it the signs of their affection or their anger, warming it with their summer breath or biting it with their icy teeth. But because I was polished by the wind, shaken for more than an hour, numbed by its force, I became unconscious of the shape of my body.[7]

In *L'Etranger* Meursault's descriptions of the sun's stifling heat create a strong sense of oppression, while his descriptions of a summer evening's sounds heard from his balcony evoke a feeling of the particular peace and contentment of a Mediterranean dusk. Some of the most powerful passages in *La Peste* describe the force of the plague as a combination of wind and sun beating down the defences of Oran's citizens.

Camus's physical descriptions are also remarkable for their evocation of particular places. In "La Femme adultère" and "L'Hôte" he brings the Algerian landscape to life with a few striking details: sandstorms seen through the window of a bus, tents and dromedaries in the distance, the sun melting the snow of the southern plateau.

The garishness and dampness of Amsterdam are marvellously captured in *La Chute*, even as they are filtered through Clamence's baroque prose:

> They [the Dutch burghers] walk along with us, to be sure, and yet see where their heads are: in that fog compounded of neon, gin, and peppermint emanating from the red and green shop-signs above them. . . . And night and day that dream is peopled with Lohengrins like these, dreamily riding their black bicycles with high handle-bars, funereal swans constantly drifting throughout the whole country, around the seas, along the canals.[8]

If *La Peste* begins in the manner of an historical chronicle with a deliberately flat statement of fact, Camus's other novels have remarkably brilliant first sentences that immediately set the mood and begin the action. In *L'Etranger* Meursault comments laconically on his mother's death: "Mother died today. Or, maybe, yesterday; I can't be sure."[9] In *La Chute* Clamence introduces himself in a smooth, insinuating manner:

> May I, Monsieur, offer my services without running the risk of intruding? I fear you may not be able to make yourself understood by the worthy gorilla who presides over the fate of this establishment.[10]

Camus had a fine eye for exact detail; he was often a brilliant caricaturist. Salamano in *L'Etranger* drags his mangy dog down the street without stopping when the dog urinates. In *La Peste* Grand continually revises the opening sentence of his novel; a whole concept of life is conveyed by the old asthma patient's gesture of transferring dried peas from one pot to another.

If in Camus's fiction there are no characters who are analysed in great depth, it is because modern authors often doubt their ability to comprehend the minds of others or to portray a reality that is always shifting.

Camus, however, creates for each of his narrators an individual idiom and point of view. His heroes have private inner lives that are not described directly, but are subtly indicated in the way they speak. The psychological pressures upon Meursault are shown by the variations in the rhythms of his sentences, by his recourse to poetic imagery when he cannot understand what is happening (as in the murder scene on the beach), and by his deliberate attention to detail during moments of stress. (He avoids becoming emotionally disturbed at his mother's funeral by studying the nails in her coffin.)

If Meursault, despite the pressures on him, is fundamentally at ease in life, Dr Rieux, the narrator of *La Peste*, is less secure. Rieux's idiom and his method of telling his story indicate a basic distrust of the world and of his fellow men. He is over cautious in his choice of words and he qualifies all general statements; although he judges other men ironically, he tries to describe them in a favourable light. As a result his prose style is often awkward, conveying an impression of unresolved inner tension.

In the tone of Clamence's speeches, Camus has created an accurate echo of modern cynicism. Clamence is ironic and mocking in his judgments of others; he coins striking, bitter aphorisms. His language is cleverly satiric and his style is polished and literary. If Meursault writes in a non-literary tense (the *passé composé*), Clamence uses outmoded subjunctive verb forms in his speech. The extreme fluency and elegance of his language convey a feeling that he has something to hide, that he looks for stylistic grace to compensate for his inner distress.

In his novels Camus uses varying narrative techniques to establish character. Meursault writes in the first-person and yet remains detached from his narrative; Rieux hides behind anonymity; Clamence uses his monologue as a means of self-display. The stories in *L'Exil et le royaume* may be considered as further experiments in this direction. Camus varies the narrative point of view and style to catch the distinct features of each character and to suggest both the hero's relationship to society and his psychological tensions. The renegade priest in "Le Renégat" speaks in confused syntactical patterns and uses images of pain and punishment. His monologue is the product of a disordered mind. In "La Femme adultère" and "L'Hôte" the protagonists' psychological tensions are suggested by the alternations between flat matter-of-fact statements and densely metaphoric passages. The characters are torn between accepting their conventional social roles and seeking a solitary contentment in the natural world.

Although his plays are of secondary value, Camus has a permanent place in French literature as an essayist and novelist. While *La Peste* is flawed by a certain rigidity and *La Chute* is over abstract, *L'Etranger* is totally successful, a classic novel. If Camus's novels are less satisfying than those of such early twentieth-century giants as Proust or Gide, they are still the finest fiction of his generation. He came as close as was possible to expressing with integrity the difficult experiences of an age that saw its moral values shattered and that needed to rebuild a faith in man's dignity.

REFERENCES

1. Robert Kanters, "Camus: Prince des bien pensants ou de la révolte?" (1962), pp. 32–3.

2. Carl Viggiani, "Camus' L'Etranger" (1956), p. 871.

3. Gaëtan Picon, Review of L'Exil et le royaume (1957), p. 154.

4. Pierre-Henri Simon, Présence de Camus (1961), p. 50.

5. Angus Wilson, "Albert Camus, Humanist" (1960), p. 293.

6. Irving Howe, "Between Fact and Fable" (1958), p. 17.

7. N., p. 32.

8. C., pp. 18–19 (12).

9. E., p. 9 (11).

10. C., p. 7 (5).

BIBLIOGRAPHY

*In all cases in which two or more editions of any work are
listed, all references in the text are to the editions marked * in
this Bibliography.*

I. CAMUS

1. Collected Works

Collected Fiction. Translations of the novels and short stories, published
in one volume, London (Hamish Hamilton) 1960.

Albert Camus: Théâtre, récits, nouvelles. Paris (Gallimard) 1962. Includes
plays, novels, and stories, with notes by Roger Quilliot.

2. Novels and Short Stories

L'Etranger. Paris (Gallimard) 1942. Eng. translation: *The Outsider*, tr.
Stuart Gilbert, London (Hamish Hamilton) 1946; *new edn.,
London (Hamish Hamilton) 1957; *The Stranger*, tr. Stuart
Gilbert, New York (Knopf) 1946, and Vintage edn.

La Peste. Paris (Gallimard) 1947. Eng. translation: *The Plague*, tr.
Stuart Gilbert, *London (Hamish Hamilton) and New York
(Knopf) 1948. Also in Modern Library edn.

La Chute. Paris (Gallimard) 1956. Eng. translation: *The Fall*, tr.
Justin O'Brien, *London (Hamish Hamilton) and New York
(Knopf) 1957, and Vintage edn.

L'Exil et le royaume. Paris (Gallimard) 1957. Eng. translation: *Exile
and the Kingdom*, tr. Justin O'Brien, *London (Hamish Hamilton)
and New York (Knopf) 1958.

3. Plays and Translations

La Révolte dans les Asturies. Algiers (Charlot) 1936. Written in col-
laboration with others.

Le Malentendu and *Caligula.* Paris (Gallimard) 1945. *Revised edn.,
Paris (Gallimard) 1958. Eng. translation: *Caligula* and *Cross
Purposes,* tr. Stuart Gilbert, *London (Hamish Hamilton) and
New York (New Directions) 1947. Also in *Caligula and Three
Other Plays* (as *The Misunderstanding*), New York (Knopf) 1958,
and Vintage edn. 1962.

L'Etat de siège. Paris (Gallimard) 1948. Eng. translation in *Caligula
and Three Other Plays*, tr. Stuart Gilbert, New York (Knopf) 1958.

Les Justes. Paris (Gallimard) 1950. Eng. translation in *Caligula and
Three Other Plays*, tr. Stuart Gilbert, New York (Knopf) 1958.

La Dévotion à la Croix. Translation of Pedro Calderón: *La devoción de la
Cruz.* Paris (Gallimard) 1953.

Adaptation of Pierre de Larivey: *Les Esprits*. Paris (Gallimard) 1953.

"La Vie d'artiste: Mimodrame en deux parties," in *Simoun* (Oran), II (1953), pp. 14–20. A mime from which the theme of "Jonas" was later developed.

Requiem pour une nonne. Adaptation of William Faulkner: *Requiem for a Nun*. Paris (Gallimard) 1956.

Le Chevalier d'Olmédo. Translation of Lope de Vega: *El Caballero de Olmedo*. Paris (Gallimard) 1957.

Les Possédés. Adaptation of Dostoevsky: *The Possessed*. Paris (Gallimard) 1959. Eng. translation: *The Possessed*, tr. Justin O'Brien, London (Hamish Hamilton) and New York (Knopf) 1960.

4. Philosophical, Political and Lyrical Essays

L'Envers et l'endroit. Algiers (Charlot) 1937. *New edn. with a preface by Camus, Paris (Gallimard) 1958.

Noces. Algiers (Charlot) 1938. *New edn., Paris (Gallimard) 1947. One essay translated in *The Myth of Sisyphus*, tr. Justin O'Brien.

Le Mythe de Sisyphe. Paris (Gallimard) 1942. *New edn. with an added study of Franz Kafka, Paris (Gallimard) 1945. Eng. translation: *The Myth of Sisyphus* tr. Justin O'Brien, *London (Hamish Hamilton) and New York (Knopf) and Vintage edn. 1955. This volume also contains essays in translation from *Noces* ("Summer in Algiers"), *L'Eté* ("The Minotaur or The Stop in Oran," "Helen's Exile," and "Return to Tipasa") and *Actuelles II* ("The Artist and His Time").

Lettres à un ami allemand. Paris (Gallimard) 1945. Eng. translation in *Resistance, Rebellion and Death*, tr. Justin O'Brien.

Actuelles: Chroniques, 1944–1948. Paris (Gallimard) 1950. Selections translated in *Resistance, Rebellion and Death*.

L'Homme révolté. Paris (Gallimard) 1951. Eng. translation, *The Rebel*, tr. Anthony Bower, *London (Hamish Hamilton) 1953; New York (Knopf) 1954, and Vintage edn.

Actuelles II: Chroniques, 1948–1953. Paris (Gallimard) 1953. Selections translated in *Resistance, Rebellion and Death*.

L'Eté. Paris (Gallimard) 1954. Essays written between 1939 and 1953. Three essays translated in *The Myth of Sisyphus*, tr. Justin O'Brien.

"Réflexions sur la guillotine," in *Réflexions sur la peine capitale*, with Arthur Koestler, Paris (Calmann-Lévy) 1957. Eng. translation in *Resistance, Rebellion and Death*.

Discours de Suède. Paris (Gallimard) 1958. Nobel Prize acceptance speech. Eng. translation in *Resistance, Rebellion and Death*.

Actuelles III: Chronique algérienne, 1939–1958. Paris (Gallimard) 1958. Selections translated in *Resistance, Rebellion and Death*.

Resistance, Rebellion and Death. *London (Hamish Hamilton) 1961 ; New York (Knopf) 1960. Translated and with an Introduction by Justin O'Brien. Contains *Letters to a German Friend*, articles from the three volumes of *Actuelles*, the Nobel Prize speech, "Reflections on the Guillotine," and several interviews from newspapers.

Carnets: Mai 1935–Février 1942. Paris (Gallimard) 1962. First published volume of Camus's notebooks. Eng. translation: *Carnets 1935–1942*, tr. Philip Thody, London (Hamish Hamilton) 1963. *Notebooks, 1935–42*, tr. Philip Thody, New York (Knopf) 1963.

5. Miscellaneous Articles

"L'Intelligence et l'échafaud," in *Confluences*, special number entitled "Problèmes du roman," ed. Jean Prévost, Jul.–Aug. 1943, pp. 218–23.

"Remarque sur la révolte," in *L'Existence*, ed. Jean Grenier, Paris (Gallimard) 1945.

"Preface" to René Leynaud: *Poésies posthumes*. Paris (Gallimard) 1947, pp. 7–18.

"L'Artiste en prison." Preface to Oscar Wilde: *La Ballade de la geôle de Reading*, Paris (Gallimard) 1952. Eng. translation: "The Artist in Prison," tr. Antonia White, in *Encounter* II, No. 3 (1954), pp. 26–9.

"Herman Melville," in *Les Ecrivains célèbres*, VOL. II, ed. Raymond Queneau, Paris (Mazenod) 1952, pp. 128–9.

"Foreword" to Louis Guilloux: *La Maison du peuple*. Paris (Gallimard) 1953.

"Lettre à Barthes sur *La Peste*," in *Club* (Bulletin du club du meilleur livre), Feb. 1955, p. 7.

"Preface" to school's edn. of *L'Etranger*, New York (Vintage Books) 1955; London (Methuen) 1958. *Reprinted in *La Nouvelle nouvelle revue française*, XI (1958), pp. 547–8.

"Preface" to Roger Martin du Gard: *Oeuvres complètes*. Paris (Gallimard) 1955.

"Lettre au sujet du *Parti pris*," in *La Nouvelle nouvelle revue français* VIII (1956), pp. 386–92.

"Parties and Truth," in *Encounter*, No. 43 (Apr. 1957), pp. 3–5. Interview reprinted from *Tempo Presente*.

"The Lie and the Quarter-Truth," in *The Observer*, 17 Nov. 1957, p .16.

"Pages de carnets," in *Symposium*, XII (1958), pp. 1–6. Selections from Camus's notebooks for Apr. 1941 and Dec. 1942.

"Preface" to Jean Grenier: *Les Iles*. Paris (Gallimard) 1959, pp. 9–16.

Interview with Robert Donald Spector, in *Venture*, III (1960), pp. 25–39. Answers to a questionnaire written by Camus in Dec. 1959, very shortly before his death.

II. OTHERS

1. In English

AURY, DOMINIQUE: "Talk with Albert Camus," in *New York Times Book Review*, 17 Feb. 1957, p. 33.

AYER, A. J.: "Novelist-Philosophers," in *Horizon*, XIII (1946), pp. 155–168.

BERTOCCI, ANGELO P.: "Camus' *La Peste* and the Absurd," in *Romanic Review*, XLIX (1958), pp. 33–41.

BRÉE, GERMAINE: *Camus*, New Brunswick 1958.

——, ed.: *Camus: A Collection of Critical Essays*, Englewood Cliffs 1962.

BROWN, NORMAN O.: *Life Against Death*, New York 1959.

CONNOLLY, CYRIL: "Introduction" to *The Outsider*, London 1946. *New edn. 1957, pp. 5–10.

CRUICKSHANK, JOHN: *Albert Camus and the Literature of Revolt*, Oxford 1959.

FROHOCK, W. M.: "Camus: Image, Influence and Sensibility," in *Yale French Studies*, II (1949), pp. 91–9.

GALPIN, ALFRED: "Dante in Amsterdam," in *Symposium*, XII (1958), pp. 65–72.

HALL, H. GASTON: "Aspects of the Absurd," in *Yale French Studies*, No. 25 (1960), pp. 26–32.

HANNA, THOMAS: *The Thought and Art of Albert Camus*, Chicago 1958.

HOWE, IRVING: "Between Fact and Fable," in *New Republic*, 31 Mar. 1958, pp. 17–18.

HUDON, LOUIS: "*The Stranger* and the Critics," in *Yale French Studies*, No. 25 (1960), pp. 59–64.

JOHN, S.: "Image and Symbol in the Work of Albert Camus," in *French Studies*, IX (1955), pp. 42–53.

KING, ADELE: "Structure and Meaning in *La Chute*," in *Publications of the Modern Language Association*, LXXVII (1962), pp. 660–7.

LEWIS, R. W. B.: *The Picaresque Saint: Representative Figures in Contemporary Fiction*, Philadelphia 1959.

MASON, H. A.: "Albert Camus: Difficult Hope," in *Scrutiny*, XIV (1947), pp. 306–12.

MOHRT, MICHEL: "Ethic and Poetry in the Work of Camus," in *Yale French Studies*, I (1948), pp. 113–18.

ROSSI, LOUIS R.: "Albert Camus: The Plague of Absurdity," in *Kenyon Review*, XX (1958), pp. 399–422.

STOURZH, GERALD: "The Unforgivable Sin: An Interpretation of *The Fall*," in *Chicago Review*, XV (1961), pp. 45–57.

THODY, PHILIP: *Albert Camus*, London 1957.

——: *Albert Camus: 1913–1960*, London 1961.

ULLMANN, STEPHEN: "The two styles of Camus," in *The Image in the Modern French Novel*, Cambridge 1960, pp. 239–99.

VIGGIANI, CARL A.: "Camus' *L'Etranger*," in *Publications of the Modern Language Association*, LXXI (1956), pp. 865–87.

——: "Camus in 1936: The Beginnings of a Career," in *Symposium*, XII (1958), pp. 7–18.

——: "Albert Camus' First Publications," in *Modern Language Notes*, LXXV (1960), pp. 589–96.

WEINBURG, KURT: "The Theme of Exile," in *Yale French Studies*, No. 25 (1960), pp. 33–40.

WILSON, ANGUS: "Albert Camus, Humanist," in *The Spectator*, 26 Feb. 1960, p. 293. Also published in French in *La Nouvelle revue française*, No. 87 (1960), pp. 545–8.

2. In French and German

A *Albert Camus, ses amis du livre*, Paris 1962. Reminiscences of type-setters and proof-readers who worked with Camus.

BEAUVOIR, SIMONE DE: *Les Mandarins*, Paris 1954.

BESPALOFF, RACHEL: "Le monde du condamné à mort," in *Esprit*, No. 163 (1950), pp. 1–26.

PANCHOT, MAURICE: "La Confession dédaigneuse," in *La Nouvelle nouvelle revue française*, VIII (1956), pp. 1050–6.

BLOCH-MICHEL, JEAN: "Albert Camus et la nostalgie de l'innocence," in *Preuves*, No. 110 (1960), pp. 3–9.

BONNIER, HENRY: *Albert Camus ou la force d'être*, Lyon and Paris 1959.

BRISVILLE, JEAN-CLAUDE: *Camus*, Paris 1959.

CHAMPIGNY, ROBERT: *Sur un héros païen*, Paris 1959.

CHAUVIRÉ, JACQUES: *Les Passants*, Paris 1961.

CRÉPIN, SIMONE: *Albert Camus: Essai de bibliographie*, Brussels 1960.

DANIEL, JEAN: "Albert Camus, parlons de lui . . . ," in *L'Express*, 7 Jan. 1960, pp. 27–9.

DURAND, ANNE: *Le Cas Albert Camus*, Paris 1961.

ETIEMBLE: "Peste ou péché," in *Les Temps modernes*, III (1947), pp. 911–20.

HEURGON, JACQUES: "Jeunesse de la Méditerranée," in *La Table ronde*, No. 146 (1960), pp. 16–21.

HOUDIN, GEORGES: *Camus le juste*, Paris 1960.

JEANSON, FRANCIS: "Albert Camus ou l'âme révoltée," in *Les Temps modernes*, VII (1952), pp. 2070–90.

——: "Pour tout vous dire . . . ," in *Les Temps modernes*, VIII (1952), pp. 354–83.

KANTERS, ROBERT: "Camus: Prince des bien pensants ou de la révolte?" in *L'Express*, 3 May 1962, pp. 32–3.

LUPPÉ, ROBERT DE: *Albert Camus*, Paris 1957.

MAQUET, ALBERT: *Albert Camus ou l'invincible été*, Paris 1956.

MATTHEWS, J. H.: "L'Oeil de Meursault," in "Configuration Critique d'Albert Camus, I," *Revue des lettres modernes*, VIII (1961), pp. 137–149.

MOELLER, CHARLES: "La Pauvreté et la lumière," in *La Table ronde*, No. 146 (1960), pp. 103–13.

NÉGRONI, JEAN: "Albert Camus et le théâtre de l'équipe," in *Revue d'histoire du théâtre*, IV (1960), pp. 343–9.

NOYER-WEIDNER, ALFRED: "Das Formproblem der 'Pest' von Albert Camus," in *Germanisch-Romanische Monatsschrift*, VIII (1958), pp. 260–85.

PICON, GAËTAN: "Remarques sur *La Peste*," in *Fontaine*, No. 61 (1947), pp. 453–60.

——: Review of *La Chute*, in *Le Mercure de France*, Aug. 1956, pp. 688–93.

——: Review of *L'Exil et le royaume*, in *Le Mercure de France*, May 1957, pp. 127–31. *Eng. translation in *Camus*, ed. Germaine Brée, Englewood Cliffs 1962, pp. 152–6.

POUILLON, J.: "L'Optimisme de Camus," in *Les Temps modernes*, III (1947), pp. 921–9.

QUILLIOT, ROGER: *La Mer et les prisons*, Paris 1956.

——: "Un monde ambigu," in *Preuves*, No. 110 (1960), pp. 28–38.

RENAUD, ARMAND: "Quelques remarques sur le style de *L'Etranger*," in *French Review*, XXX (1956–7), pp. 290–6.

ROBBE-GRILLET, ALAIN: "Nature, humanisme, tragédie," in *La Nouvelle nouvelle revue française*, XII (1958), pp. 580–604.

ROBLÈS, EMMANUEL: "Jeunesse d'Albert Camus," in *La Nouvelle revue française*, No. 87 (1960), pp. 410–21.

SARTRE, JEAN-PAUL: "Explication de *L'Etranger*," in *Situations I*, Paris 1947, pp. 91–121.

——: *Situations II: Qu'est-ce que la littérature?*, Paris 1948.

——: "Réponse à Albert Camus," in *Les Temps modernes*, VIII (1952), pp. 334–54.

SIMON, PIERRE-HENRI: *Présence de Camus*, Paris 1961.

Soleil noir, No. 1 (1952). "La Révolte en question." Issue devoted to an attack on *L'Homme révolté*.

THODY, PHILIP: "Meursault et la critique," in "Configuration critique d'Albert Camus, I," *Revue des lettres modernes*, VIII (1961), pp. 11–22.

THOORENS, LÉON: *A la rencontre d'Albert Camus*, Paris 1946.

TILLION, GERMAINE: "Devant le malheur algérien," in *Preuves*, No. 110 (1960), pp. 25–7.

VIGÉE, CLAUDE: "La Nostalgie du sacré chez Albert Camus," in *La Nouvelle revue française*, No. 87 (1960), pp. 527–36.

——: "L'Errance entre l'exil et le royaume," in *La Table ronde*, No. 146 (1960), pp. 120–6.